A+ Certification
Troubleshooting and Repair
Pocket Guide

Joe Froehlich

A+ Certification Troubleshooting and Repair Pocket Guide

Part Number: 085811   Course Edition: 1.1

ACKNOWLEDGMENTS

Project Team

Editor: Joe Froehlich • **Copy Editors:** Jeff Hotchkiss and Christine Hunt • **Graphic Designer:** Amy Palermo

NOTICES

The logo of the CompTIA Authorized Curriculum Program and the status of this or other training material as "Authorized" under the CompTIA Authorized Curriculum Program signifies that, in CompTIA's opinion, such training material covers the content of the CompTIA's related certification exam. CompTIA has not reviewed or approved the accuracy of the contents of this training material and specifically disclaims any warranties of merchantability or fitness for a particular purpose. CompTIA makes no guarantee concerning the success of persons using any such "Authorized" or other training material in order to prepare for any CompTIA certification exam. The contents of this training material were created for the CompTIA A+ exam covering CompTIA certification exam objectives that were current as of April, 2003.

How to Become CompTIA Certified: This training material can help you prepare for and pass a related CompTIA certification exam or exams. In order to achieve CompTIA certification, you must register for and pass a CompTIA certification exam or exams. In order to become CompTIA certified, you must:

1. Select a certification exam provider. For more information please visit http://www.comptia.org/certification/genral_information/test_locations.asp.
2. Register for and schedule a time to take the CompTIA certification exam(s) at a convenient location.
3. Read and sign the Candidate Agreement, which will be presented at the time of the exam(s). The text of the Candidate Agreement can be found at http://www.comptia.org/certification/general_ information/candidate_agreement.asp.
4. Take and pass the CompTIA certification exam(s).

For more information about CompTIA's certifications, such as their industry acceptance, benefits, or program news, please visit http://www.comptia.org/certification/default.asp. CompTIA is a non-profit information technology (IT) trade association. CompTIA's certifications are designed by subject matter experts from across the IT industry. Each CompTIA certification is vendor-neutral, covers multiple technologies, and requires demonstration of skills and knowledge widely sought after by the IT industry. To contact CompTIA with any questions or comments: Please call + 1 630 268 1818 questions@comptia.org

Table of Contents

Introduction

by Joe Froehlich, A+, Network+, I-Net+, CNA, MCP, ACTC

A+ Certification Troubleshooting and Repair Pocket Guide is a concise reference of support information that you can use on the job. It combines the technical information you'll use to answer your clients' questions with the technical support procedures you put into practice to maintain their equipment. The guide is organized into five sections to help you find the facts and techniques you'll refer to during your workday:

- Section I: Troubleshooting Methodology

- Section II: Supporting Computer Hardware

- Section III: Supporting Computer Operating Systems

- Section IV. Supporting Computer Networks

- Section V: Customer Care

In **Section I: Troubleshooting Methodology**, we look at a general approach to isolating and solving computer problems. Then, we review techniques for safely repairing, upgrading, and maintaining computer systems.

In **Section II: Supporting Computer Hardware**, we examine the basic hardware common to most computers. After a detailed look at the motherboard and the power supply, we show you how to install internal and external components. Finally, we concentrate on portable computers and their special requirements.

In **Section III: Supporting Computer Operating Systems**, we concentrate first on the boot process and the diagnostic options that are available during the process. Then, we look at ways to recover from major software disasters. Next, we look at system upgrade options, a common solution to many software and hardware problems. Lastly, we look at malicious software and the ways you can protect a computer from viruses.

In **Section IV: Supporting Computer Networks**, we discuss basic network layouts and connections. After going over Ethernet connections in detail, we outline the facts you need to choose the right Internet connection.

In **Section V: Customer Care**, we present ways to gauge your professional conduct and to scrutinize your professional behavior. No matter how good you are technically, you need customers in order for you to stay in business. We'll show you how to exceed your customers' expectations.

We hope you find *A+ Certification Troubleshooting and Repair Pocket Guide* a valuable addition to your support library. Read through it to review the main concepts important to computer support professionals. Carry it with you when you're on the job, and you'll be prepared for most support challenges you'll encounter.

Section I: Troubleshooting Methodology

Troubleshooting can be a daunting task for a computer service professional. Certainly, you must have extensive knowledge of both hardware and software in order to perform the repair. However, you must also have excellent customer interaction skills so you can elicit symptoms of the problem and find the right solution. In fact, it's often said that effective troubleshooting involves 25 percent technical skills and 75 percent communication skills. When you combine the science of troubleshooting (technical skills) with the art of troubleshooting (communication skills), you can solve computer problems efficiently and effectively. Let's take a look at how you can approach any computer problem in an organized, methodical way.

Define the problem

Take the time to make sure you fully understand the problem. Your best source for this information is the actual customer; he's experienced the problem firsthand. Asking a few specific questions and listening carefully will help you accurately identify the problem. As you're interacting with the customer, be sure to document his responses to your questions. Some questions you might ask are as follows:

- When did you first notice the problem or error?

- Was the computer working properly before you noticed the problem?

- Did you install any new hardware or software just prior to noticing the problem?

- Exactly which task were you performing on the computer when you experienced the problem?

- Can you reproduce the problem or error? If so, how?

- Has anything happened to the computer recently? Was it moved? Was something dropped or spilled on it?

- What does the problem or error look like?

- What are the physical characteristics of the problem? Smells? Noise? Heat? Lights? Error messages?

- Do you have current backups of your applications and data files?

Once you've asked a few questions, you should examine the computer to confirm the customer's statements as much you can. When doing so, communicate your findings to the customer and assure him you'll work to resolve the problem.

Isolate the problem

Once you've compiled a list of symptoms from your customer, your job is to zero in on the problem. Start by eliminating the obvious and then work from the simplest to the more complex. Try to narrow your search down to a specific category, such as those shown in **Table 1.1** on page 12. Whenever possible, try to re-create the set of circumstances that caused the problem. You might have your customer demonstrate the failure to you. Then, try to reproduce the problem yourself to confirm that it's repeatable.

Conduct the repair

Once you've narrowed down the problem to a specific category, try to isolate the problem to a specific hardware or software component. Next, develop a plan that you can follow from beginning to end to validate your assumptions.

Before proceeding with your plan, back up the customer's system and document the current configuration. As you proceed with your plan, document every action you take and its results. Don't deviate dramatically from your original plan. Doing so may introduce other, more serious, problems. If the first plan doesn't work, design a new plan based on what you've learned from implementing the previous plan. Once you've found a solution to the problem, talk to your customer. Make sure he understands the solution you found and get his permission to proceed with the repair.

Confirm the results

No repair is complete until both you and the customer are satisfied with the results. After completing the repair, your first task should be to confirm that the problem no longer exists. Once you've completed that step, you should confirm that the repair didn't introduce a new problem. Test the system thoroughly, looking for potential side effects of the repair. Whenever possible, ask a colleague to test the solution.

Document the results

Finally, document the problem and the repair in detail. There's no substitute for experience in troubleshooting, and documentation should be part and parcel of every service you perform. Every new problem presents you with an opportunity to expand on your experience. Keeping a copy of the repair procedure in your technical library will come in handy later if the problem (or one like it) occurs again. If you maintain repair records in an electronic database, you can easily search the database to find the answers to the same problems that might arise again later. The records you keep, whether manual or electronic, will be invaluable if there are later questions about the service performed from a client or insurance company.

Table 1.1: *Categories of common computer problems*

Problem category	Typical symptoms
Power	Dead computer, intermittent errors on power-on self-test (POST), intermittent lockups, or onscreen messages, such as *Device not working* or *Device not found*.
Connectivity	Onscreen messages, such as *Device not working* or *Device not found*, intermittent errors on a device, device failure, or failure to boot.
Boot	Dead computer, consistent errors on POST, beep errors, and CMOS text errors.
Memory	Dead computer, parity errors, General Protection Fault (GPF) with consistent addresses, and HIMEM.SYS errors.
Mass storage	Onscreen error messages include: *Missing Operating System, File Not Found, No Boot Device,* and *Abort, Retry, Fail.*
Input/Output	System locks up, *Device not responding* error message received onscreen, strange or erratic behavior from a device.
Operating system	Missing operating system, bad or missing command interpreter, onscreen request to *Insert Disk with COMMAND.COM* file on it, stack overflow, or insufficient file handles.
Applications	Application doesn't work properly, application-specific errors, application-specific GPFs, or lock-ups only in specific applications.
Device drivers	Device lockups on access, intermittent lockups, or computer runs in safe mode only.
Memory management	*Not Enough Memory* error onscreen, missing extended memory specification (XMS) and expanded memory specification (EMS), device lockups, GPFs at KRNL386.EXE, and GPFs at USER.EXE or GDI.EXE.

Table 1.1: *Continued*

Problem category	Typical symptoms
Configuration/Setup	Programs refusing to do something they should, missing options in programs, missing programs, or missing devices.
Viruses	Computer runs slowly, failure to boot, intermittent lockups, storage problems, operating system problems, and other mysterious symptoms.
Network	User forgets password, user has an expired password, or cable or NIC (network interface card) problems

Section II: Supporting Computer Hardware

General procedures

While you may be looking forward to the challenge of repairing a computer, there are some procedures to follow before you start that make the process safer for you and the equipment you work on. Also, some simple maintenance practices will help you avoid major repairs in the future. Once you have done all you can to prevent future problems, you can look at ways to solve hardware-related problems on all the components found in a typical computer system.

Resetting devices and reconnecting cables

While tearing a computer apart can be fun, an amazing number of problems are solved using the steps below. While neither glamorous nor thought provoking, the following steps can save hours of time and effort:

- Turn off all the peripherals and the computer. After a minute, turn on the peripherals, turn on the computer, and see if the problem has gone away. This step resets everything and gives the computer a fresh start.

- If the problem is still there, turn off all the peripherals and the computer. Disconnect all the cables going to and from the computer and the peripherals, and then inspect and reconnect the cables securely in the proper sockets. Reboot the computer and see if the problem remains.

- If the problem is still there, then you need to move on to the procedures in Sections III and IV in this book.

Creating a safe work environment

When you're installing internal hardware components, you need to follow safe work practices to protect yourself from injury. For example, you should never attempt to repair a power supply and you should only work on CRTs if you've had special training. For most other components, follow these general safe practices:

- Unplug the AC power cord when working with the computer power supply cables and switches.

- Avoid touching heat sinks and other hot components.

- Replace the computer cover and slot filler panels before operating the computer so cooling air circulation will protect the equipment from overheating.

- Install surge protectors and an Uninterruptible Power Supply (UPS) to protect the computer against power surges and power loss.

- Operate the computer in a cool, stable, magnetism-free area.

- Use multimeter test probes cautiously so the probe tips don't create short circuits and don't damage delicate circuit paths on the circuit board.

- Protect your eyes from concentrated light found in scanners, laser printers, and CD-ROM drives.

Preventing damage from static electricity

Electronic components are extremely susceptible to electrostatic discharge (ESD). In order to avoid damaging components, use the following guidelines to create an ESD-free work environment:

- Wear an anti-static wrist strap grounded to the computer chassis to bleed harmful electrostatic charges to a safe ground.

- Leave the AC cord plugged into the wall outlet, and turn the computer off, so you have a reliable ground for your wrist strap.

- Place circuit boards, drives, chips, and other components on properly grounded anti-static mats.

- Handle printed circuit boards by the edges. Store and transport electrostatic-sensitive devices in anti-static bags.

- Avoid nylon, regular plastic, vinyl, and low humidity because they all increase the chance of electrostatic build-up.

Cleaning peripherals

Well cared for peripherals have a longer, trouble-free life span. Harsh cleaning agents can damage the peripherals, so follow these guidelines:

- Clean the keyboard using compressed air, an artist's paintbrush, a business card, toothpicks, or rubbing alcohol.

- Clean the mouse by removing the ball and cleaning the rollers with rubbing alcohol and toothpicks, and clean the mouse interior with compressed air.

- Clean the monitor by spraying glass cleaner on a lint-free cloth, and then wipe the glass. Clean the vents using a small vacuum.

- Clean PDAs using a lint-free cloth to wipe the screen and a lint-free cloth dampened with rubbing alcohol to wipe down the body of the PDA.

- Clean scanners by spraying glass cleaner on a lint-free cloth, and then wipe the glass. Wipe the exterior with a lint-free cloth dampened with household cleaner.

- Clean contacts and connections with a lint-free cloth or an artist's paintbrush.

Cleaning system components

The components inside the computer must also be clean and dust-free to function correctly. Follow these procedures to increase the life span of the computer system:

- Remove the case and clean it with a damp lint-free cloth.

- Clean the system board using a compressed air canister and computer vacuum. Try to hold the case at an angle with the back corner. Blow the air so the dust is blown away from the drives and power supply. If it is extremely dusty, you might want to wear a mask over your mouth and nose, since the dust particles will fly up when you spray the compressed air.

- Clean the CD-ROM drive using a CD-ROM cleaning kit and follow the directions that come with it.

- Use a floppy drive cleaning kit and follow the directions that come with it.

- Clean removable media drives using the cleaning kit that is compatible with the drive and follow the directions that come with it.

- Iomega Zip and Jaz drives should not be cleaned. This will damage the drives. Imation SuperDrives can be cleaned.

Maintaining the operating environment

Just because a computer is running at top speed now does not mean it will continue that way. The following maintenance tips will help keep the computer in top form:

- Keep 200–500 MB of free space on the boot hard drive for Windows swap files and temporary files.

- Periodically, delete temporary files, including temporary Internet files.

- Periodically, run a disk defragmentation program and a disk cleanup program that is compatible with your operating system.

- Use Add/Remove Programs in the Control Panel to add and delete applications, and delete outdated or unused software.

- Limit programs automatically launched in Startup to the required minimum.

- Periodically, check for updates for hardware drivers, system software, and application software.

- Limit installed hardware and software to necessary components.

- Always use a comprehensive antivirus program.

Disposing of computer equipment

All computer equipment will eventually wear out or become outdated. Check your local laws and company policies before disposing of old equipment.

- Use a data-deletion program on all drives before donating, selling, or disposing of the equipment.

- Keep records of where the equipment went, and of any costs or income from the disposal.

- Transfer the equipment to another person or division in your company.

- Donate the equipment to a school or charity directly, or to companies that repackage the items for donation to tax deductible groups.

- Check for companies that accept returns of old equipment and cartridges.

- Pay a recycler to take the equipment.

- Dispose of the equipment in method approved by the local authorities.

Collecting data about a system

After you set up a safe working environment, and maintain the equipment on a regular basis, things will still go wrong. If you work through the problem-solving methods in Section I and determine that you are dealing with a hardware problem, you will need the following information.

Classifying computer systems

Today there are several types of personal computers. Support professionals are generally required to support any of the types of computers listed here:

- Desktop computers are more broad than tall, are designed to sit on top of a desk and support a monitor, and are probably the most common type of computer in offices today.

- Minitower computers are tall and narrow. They can sit on top of the desk, on the floor, or on a shelf beneath the desk. They are common in offices and in homes.

- Laptops are small computers that can be transported anywhere. They usually weigh less than 10 pounds (in fact, many weigh under five pounds) and are preferred by travelers and those that need to easily carry their work with them to multiple locations.

- Tablets are designed to look like a writing tablet. These computers typically consist of a screen on which users can enter data using their fingers or a special pen called a stylus.

- Personal Digital Assistants (PDA) are small computers about the size of a large calculator. These computers can have much of the same functionality that desktops and laptops have, although they're often slower and have less storage space.

Identifying system components

All computer systems are a collection of hardware components that are designed to operate as a single unit. The major components of a computer system are consistent from system to system, and are as follows:

- System boards, sometimes called motherboards, are the main circuit boards in computers. System boards usually contain the CPU, BIOS, memory, I/O ports, and controllers. Slots on the system board allow the connection of additional peripheral devices.

- Input/Output (I/O) devices are hardware that transfer data to or from a computer. Input devices include keyboards and mice, output devices include printers and speakers, and combination I/O devices include hard disks and writable CD-ROMS.

- Processors, sometimes called Central Processing Units (CPU) or microprocessors, are the microcomputer chips that are the hearts and brains of personal computers. Processors are distinguished by their clock speed, bandwidth, and instruction set. Pentium and Itanium are two newer processors from Intel.

- Memory is a set of microcomputer chips inside the computer that store data. Memory on the system board is called main memory or physical memory. Many types of memory are currently in use, including Random Access Memory (RAM), Read Only Memory (ROM), Programmable Read Only Memory (PROM), and Erasable Programmable Read Only Memory (EPROM).

- Storage media include floppy disks, hard disks, and optical disks. Unlike main memory, data saved on storage media used by mass storage devices, such as hard drives and CD-ROM writers, are available after the computer is turned off.

- Interfaces are boundaries between two independent systems in a computer setup. Mice, keyboards, menus, and icons make up the user interface that lets the user communicate with the operating system. The wires, sockets, and plugs that let different computer hardware components talk to each other are hardware interfaces.

Gathering system information

Computers exist with an almost infinite number of combinations of system components. You must determine exactly what makes up a computer system before you can offer support. To do so:

- Select Start I Programs I Accessories I System Tools I System Information for a comprehensive summary of specific system information.

- Choose Help I About The Application I System Info to reach System Information from an application.

- Right-click on My Computer and select System Properties for another presentation of system resources.

- The Device Manager in System Properties not only displays information but also lets you change hardware settings.

Troubleshooting power supplies

All computers and system hardware need a reliable supply of electric power. When 100% up-time is critical, a UPS should supply the power to the computer.

- Standby Power Supply (SPS) usually supplies power to the computer directly from the power line. When the power fails, a battery-powered inverter turns on and keeps the power flowing. The batteries are constantly charged by the power line.

- Hybrid or line-interactive UPS uses a transformer to isolate and regulate the power from the power line to the computer. The battery is constantly available to upgrade the power supplied by the power line, and it takes over completely when power fails.

- True or online UPS supplies highly regulated AC power for the computer. Regular AC power is converted to DC and then back to AC so the computer power is totally isolated from the line source and all power is constantly taken from the battery. The battery is continually recharged so it can instantly take over all power requirements if power fails.

Identifying power source problems

Such problems as erratic behavior, data loss, unexplained system crashes, and even hardware damage may often be traced back to problems with the power supplied to the computer.

- Install a UPS and use shielded cables to eliminate line noise caused by Electromagnetic Interference (EMI), Radio Frequency Interference (RFI), and distant lightning strikes.

- Stagger the startup times and shutdown times of heavy equipment to reduce power sags and surges.

- Install new circuits so sufficient power is available.

- Install a UPS to protect the computer from events beyond your control, such as low voltage brownouts or a complete blackout situation caused by your electricity supplier.

Working with internal power supplies

Desktop computers have internal power supplies that convert the AC power from the wall outlet into +3.3V, +/- 5V, and +/-12V DC. Power supplies have changed form over the years to meet the needs of new motherboards and CPUs. A faulty power supply can keep the computer from turning on.

- Keep the power supply fan and all vents free of dust and debris so cooling air can circulate.

- Replace a defective power supply with one specifically designed to work with that make and model of computer. In spite of their similar appearances, power supplies from different manufacturers can differ in voltage outputs.

- ATX and SFX style power supplies are found on most desktop computers currently in use.

- ATX power supplies use a 20-pin connector to attach to the motherboard.

- Measure output voltages while the power supply is still attached to the motherboard and compare the results to the expected output for that particular make and model supply to help determine if it is defective.

- Replace, rather than attempt to repair, defective power supplies. Working on a power supply can be physically dangerous.

- Internal power supplies also energize internal adapter cards and disk drives, so the supply must be rated high enough to handle all installed components. The power rating of supplies can range for 150 watts to 600 or more watts. 300 watts or more are generally required.

- The power supply must be designed to handle the input AC voltage. In the USA, standard outlets supply 120 VAC at 60 Hz, but in other countries the outlets supply 220 VAC. Some supplies adapt to either voltage, but others can't.

- Advanced Power Management (APM) reduces total power consumption by turning down or turning off computer components after set periods of time. Some problems that seem related to power supplies may simply be power management problems.

Troubleshooting internal components

Many versions of motherboards are available, and new ones constantly appear. The diagram below is a typical motherboard found in today's computers.

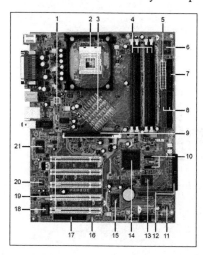

1. ATX 12V connector
2. CPU socket
3. North Bridge controller
4. DDR DIMM sockets
5. ATX power connector
6. Super I/O controller
7. Floppy disk controller
8. IDE connectors
9. AGP slot
10. Serial ATA connectors
11. Speech controller
12. RAID Ultra ATA/133 connector
13. Flash ROM
14. South Bridge controller
15. ATA 133 RAID controller
16. Standby Power LED

17. WiFi slot
18. 1394 controller
19. PCI slots
20. Audio CODEC
21. Gigabit LAN controller
22. PS/2 mouse
23. Parallel port
24. IEEE 1394 port
25. RJ-45 port
26. Line In jack
27. Line Out jack
28. Microphone jack
29. USB 2.0 ports 3 and 4

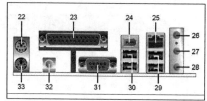

30. USB 2.0 ports 1 and 2
31. Serial port
32. S/PDIF output port
33. Keyboard port

Identifying motherboard form factors

Motherboard form factors, like those in **Table 2.1**, determine the general shape of the system board, the case it can fit into, the power supply it needs, and its physical organization. When upgrading a motherboard, the replacement must have the same form factors as the original to fit in the case and work with the old power supply.

Identifying CPUs

CPU chips are the heart of a computer system. **Table 2.2** lists significant CPUs that helped shape the PC in-

Table 2.1: Motherboard form factors

Style	Width	Depth	Where found
Full AT	12"	11-13"	Very old PCs
Baby AT	8.5"	10-13"	Older PCs
ATX	12"	9.6"	Newer PCs
Mini ATX	11.2"	8.2"	Newer PCs
LPX	9"	11-13"	Older retail PCs
Mini LPX	8-9"	10-11"	Older retail PCs
NLX	8-9"	10-13.6"	Newer retail PCs

Table 2.2: Common busses and their theoretical throughput

Processor	Year	Data bus	Typical speeds	Maximum memory
8088	1979	8-bit	4.77 MHz	1 MB
8086	1978	16-bit	5, 6, 8, and 10 MHz	1 MB
286	1982	16-bit	8, 10, and 12.5 up to 20 MHz	16 MB
386SX	1988	16-bit	16 to 33 MHz	16 MB
386DX	1985	32-bit	16, 20, 25, and 33 MHz	4 GB
486/AMD-5x86	1989	32-bit	25, 33, 50, and 66 MHz	4 GB

dustry. While most of the list is from Intel, companies like Motorola, AMD, and Cyrix also produce CPUs. Computers with these CPUs are good candidates for immediate replacement.

Starting with the Pentium, the CPUs used a 64-bit data bus. Itanium 2 has a 128-bit data bus. The newer the CPU, the more calculations it can do per second, and the faster it can transmit that information, as shown in **Table 2.3**.

The Pentium family of CPUs uses a variety of sockets on the motherboard, as shown in **Table 2.4** on the next page. Each socket has a special Pin Grid Array (PGA) or Staggered Pin Grid Array (SPGA) that accepts a limited number of CPUs.

Table 2.3: *Modern CPU specifications*

CPU	Core speed	Bus speed	Maximum memory
Pentium	75–200 MHz	50–66 MHz	4 GB
Pentium Pro	150–200 MHz	60–66 MHz	64 GB
Pentium with MMX	150–266 MHz	66 MHz	4 GB
Pentium II	233–400 MHz	66–100 MHz	64 GB
Pentium II Xeon	400–450 MHz	100 MHz	64 GB
Celeron	266 MHz–2 GHz	66–400 MHz	64 GB
Pentium III	533 MHz–1.4 GHz	100–133 MHz	64 GB
Pentium III Xeon	500 MHz–1 GHz	100–133 MHz	64 GB
Pentium 4	1.32–8 GHz	400–533 MHz	64 GB
Xeon	1.42–8 GHz	400 MHz	64 GB
Itanium 2	1 GHz +	400 MHz	16 TB

Zero Insertion Force (ZIF) and Low Insertion Force (LIF) sockets protect the pins on the CPU. A replacement CPU must both fit into the available socket and be compatible with the supporting hardware.

Diagnosing motherboard problems

If your peripherals and components work on other machines, but not with a specific system board, chances are excellent the problem is related to the system board. Replacing, rather than repairing, the system board is the most common

Table 2.4: *System board CPU sockets for Pentium class CPUs*

Socket type	Pin layout	Processor used
Socket 4	273-pin inline, arranged in 21 x 21 PGA grid	5v Pentium 60 and 66
Socket 5	320-pin staggered, arranged in 37 x 37 SPGA grid	3.3v early Pentium
Socket 6	235-pin inline, arranged in 19 x 19 PGA grid	3.3v 486DX4
Socket 7	321-pin staggered, arranged in 37 x 37 SPGA grid	Later Pentium, AMD K6, Cyrix 6x86, IDT
Socket 7	321-pin staggered, arranged in 37 x 37 SPGA grid	AMD K62 and K63
Socket 8	387-pin staggered ZIF, arranged in 24 x 26 SPGA grid	3.3v Pentium Pro
Socket 370	Supports PPGA	Original Celeron
Socket 423	SPGA	Pentium 4
Socket 478	SPGA	Pentium 4
Socket A	Supports PPGA	AMD Athlon, Duron, Palomino, and Morgan

solution to system board problems. Before replacing the system board, check for other possible problems:

- Trace your power supply from the wall socket to the system board and make sure all connections are secure and functional. Without reliable power, a good system board will malfunction.

- Check the CMOS settings for accuracy. Replace the CMOS battery if information is lost.

- Run a memory check to ensure memory settings are correct and that installed memory is reliable.

- Virus-check the computer.

- Update the BIOS and all applications and the operating system.

- Check that attempts to diagnose the problem have not introduced new problems, such as a cracked system board, loose screws shorting components, or misaligned cases making contact with boards.

- Clean all the heat sinks and air circulation paths, and check the fan so the CPU is not overheating.

Understanding chipsets
The chip set on a motherboard is a group of compatible, integrated circuit chips that work together to support a specific CPU. The chip set used on a motherboard determines the features and functions of that the motherboard, such as the clock generator, system timer, interrupt controller, bus controller, direct memory access (DMA), keyboard controller, memory cache, external buses, and some peripherals.

- Different chip sets, combined with the same CPU, can create computers with different capabilities and price ranges.

- Intel produces hundreds of chip sets that support its CPUs. VIA Technology, Inc., Silicon Integrated System Corp (SiS), and ALi also manufacture popular chip sets. Drivers and updates must be matched to the specific chip set in the computer.

- Peripherals, such as modems, may have a specific chip set that controls the modem. Many manufacturers may use the same chip set in their modems.

Introducing the BIOS and CMOS

CMOS (Complementary Metal Oxide Semiconductor) is a style of integrated circuit that uses very little power. In a PC, the CMOS refers to a specific chip that stores the date, time, and system hardware configuration information. A small battery supplies power to the chip so the data remains available even after the computer is shut down. CMOS support is covered in detail in **Section IV**.

Basic Input/Output System (BIOS) runs when the computer is first turned out. The BIOS uses information stored in the CMOS to set up the basic hardware, such as the hard disk, memory, video, keyboard, and the mouse. The BIOS runs initial tests on your computer, and then loads key parts of the operating system in memory. The BIOS helps your operating system and applications talk to the hardware installed on your computer. BIOS support is also covered in detail in **Section IV**, along with the entire boot-up sequence.

Solving memory problems

RAM memory consists of multiple memory integrated circuits that are positioned on circuit boards. These memory boards are inserted into memory expansion slots on the motherboard. Memory modules come in a variety of sizes and can hold different types of memory chips:

- DRAM is Dynamic Random Access Memory.

- SRAM is Static Random Access Memory, which is much faster than DRAM and is used by the CPU to cache data.

- SDRAM is Synchronous Dynamic Random Access Memory. SDRAM is DRAM that also caches or stores data so it is available the next time the CPU requests it.

- SIMMs are Single Inline Memory Modules found in older machines. SIMMs will not work in new machines. SIMMs have 30 or 72 pins.

- DIMMs are Dual Inline Memory Modules with memory names like PC100 and PC133. DIMMs have 168 pins.

- DDR DIMMs are Double Data Rate DIMMs with names like PC2100 and PC2700. DDR DIMMS have 184 pins.

- RIMMs are Rambus Inline Memory Modules found in new machines with high-end Pentium processors. They are more expensive and up to 8 times faster than DIMMs. RIMMs, sometimes called RDRAM, also have 184 pins, but in a unique arrangement. RIMMs require that all slots be filled with real memory or C-RIMMs, which just fill up empty sockets.

By installing memory designed for use on the motherboard, you will avoid unbootable computers, POST beep codes, blank screens, and numerous other problems.

- Replace or add memory that is identical to the current memory type in the machine. Do not mix memory types or speeds unless the computer manual specifically states that this is possible.

- Add or replace memory in a portable computer with memory made specifically for that make and model. Portables have stricter memory requirements than desktops.

- Replace low-capacity memory modules with higher capacity memory modules of the same type and speed if all memory slots are currently full.

- Line up the notches in the memory modules with the notches in the slot when installing memory. Use all the clasps to hold the module securely in place.

- Remove all the memory modules and replace them one at a time if the computer reports memory errors. When the error message appears again, the most recently inserted module contains the defective memory.

- Test for faulty memory if the computer crashes frequently, reboots itself, or produces General Protection Faults (GPF).

- Avoid overheating, electrostatic discharge, and power fluctuations—the most common reasons for memory failure.

Installing adapter cards

A system board contains several busses that are used to transfer data between an add-in card, main memory, and the chip set. As shown in **Table 2.5**, the product of the bus width (in bytes) and its clock frequency (in MHz) determines its throughput (in MBps).

Current adapter cards use Plug and Play (PnP) technology so the computer automatically does most of the setup for you. Adapter cards and devices usually come with an installation disk or CD-ROM that guides you through the entire process.

- Insert the new card firmly into an appropriate expansion slot and replace the computer cover so no part of the cover contacts the new card.

- Test the card on other computers to determine if the card is bad, or if a slot on your computer has gone bad if the card fails to work as expected.

Table 2.5: Common busses and their theoretical throughput

Bus	Bits per line per cycle	Width (bits)	Width (bytes)	Speed (MHz)	Throughput (MBps)
ISA (XT)	1	8	1	8.33	8.33
ISA (AT)	1	16	2	8.33	16.66
EISA	1	32	4	8.33	33.33
VLB	1	32	4	33.33	133.33
PCI	1	32	4	33.33	133.33
PCI	1	64	8	66.66	533.33
AGP 1X	1	32	4	66.66	266.66
AGP 2X	2	32	4	66.66	533.33
AGP 4X	4	32	4	66.66	1066.66
AGP 8X	8	32	4	66.66	2133.33

- Check cable connections and swap cables if the card tests fine but fails to work.

- Check resources used by the card for conflicts with other cards in the Device Manager section of System Properties. Older adapter cards are often hard-wired to use specific resources and are a source of problems when used with newer cards. New motherboards may lack slots compatible with older cards.

Resolving system resource problems

Modern systems support PnP, which allows the host operating system to allocate system resources to devices. If you're installing non-PnP devices, you'll need to manually configure their IRQ, I/O memory address, and DMA settings.

Table 2.6: *Common IRQ assignments*

IRQ	Typical assignment
0	System timer
1	Keyboard controller
2	Cascade to IRQ9
3	COM2, COM4
4	COM1, COM3
5	LPT2, sound card
6	Floppy disk controller
7	LPT1
8	Real Time Clock
9	Cascade to IRQ 2, network adapter
10	Available, network adapter, USB controller
11	Available, video adapter, SCSI host adapter
12	PS/2 mouse port
13	Numerical Processing Unit (NPU)
14	Primary IDE Hard Disk Controller
15	Secondary IDE Hard Disk Controller

Table 2.6 lists common IRQ assignments, **Table 2.7** lists common I/O memory address assignments, and **Table 2.8** on the next page lists common DMA setting assignments.

Troubleshooting mass storage devices

Some peripherals require an adapter or expansion card like those mentioned in the previous section, while other peripherals use cables that link directly to the motherboard. In

Table 2.7: *Common I/O addresses*

I/O Address	Typical use
130h	SCSI host adapters
140h	SCSI host adapters
170h	Secondary IDE Interface
1F0h	Primary IDE Interface
220h	Sound Blaster-type sound cards
240h	Alternate address for sound cards
278h	Assigned to LPT2 or LPT3 and generally used with IRQ 5
280h	Network Interface cards or the Aria Synthesizer
2A0h	Alternate address for NIC cards or the Aria Synthesizer
2E8h	Assigned to COM 4 and used with IRQ 3
2F8h	Assigned to COM 2 and used with IRQ 3
300h	Network Interface Card
320h	Network card, SCSI host adapter, MIDI device
330h	SCSI host adapters
340h	SCSI host adapter
360h	Network card choice
378h	The first parallel printer port (LPT1) in color systems; commonly used with IRQ 7
3BCh	The first parallel printer port (LPT1) in monochrome systems
3E8h	Assigned to COM 3 and used with IRQ 4
3F8h	Assigned to COM 1 and used with IRQ 4

this section, we'll look at devices that have more direct links to the motherboard.

Identifying types of mass storage

Many IDE devices are involved with mass storage. Because of the common interface, you can connect floppy disks, hard disks, CD-ROM drives, and tape drives to the internal IDE cables:

- Floppy disks are comparatively slow, small capacity, portable, inexpensive, and universally accepted.

- Hard disks are very fast and high capacity. Some hard disks are removable like floppies, but most are mounted inside the computer. Both hard disks and floppy disks use electromagnetism to encode data and can lose data if exposed to strong magnetic fields.

- Optical disks use lasers to read and write data. Blank disks are inexpensive. Optical disks have more storage than floppy disks, but not as much a hard disks. Some optical drives are read only, while others are read/write.

Table 2.8: *Common DMA settings*

DMA	Typical assignment
0	Unavailable; assigned internally to the system board
1	Available; used for sound cards or SCSI host adapters
2	Unavailable; assigned to the floppy disk drive
3	Available; used for sound cards, network interface cards, or SCSI host adapters
4	Available
5	Available; often used for SoundBlaster-compatible cards
6	Available
7	Available

- Tapes are inexpensive and can hold large amounts of data. Tapes don't permit random access to the data.

- Mass storage is measured in kilobytes (1,024 bytes), megabytes (1,024 kilobytes), gigabytes (1,024 megabytes), and terabytes (1,024 gigabytes).

Working with fixed disk drives

Fixed disk or hard disk drives have increased in storage capacity exponentially over the years, going from a 10 MB standard in 1981 to 100s of GB now, and soon terabyte (TB) drives will be common. Unfortunately, operating systems and interfacing standards can't keep up with the increased capacity.

- Quality of a drive is partially determined by its capacity, its access or seek time, its data transfer rate, and the size of its memory cache.

- Don't buy a drive larger than the system hardware and software can handle. Some drive makers supply software upgrades so you can use their giant drives in older machines.

- Back up everything. Have emergency boot disks, original application software, and operating system installation disks (and serial numbers) available before attempting any work with a hard disk.

- Partition new hard drives to help them run faster and to provide more flexibility for organizing data.

- Each physical disk can support up to four primary partitions or three primary partitions and one extended partition. The extended partition can support multiple logical volumes.

- The primary operating system should always be installed on the first primary partition. Some operating systems won't start up unless they're installed within the disk's first 1,024 cylinders.

- In general, you should use the partitioning utility supplied with the operating system you're installing. However, some third-party disk utilities allow you to create partitions that support a variety of file systems.

- The primary drive is usually configured as the master drive and the second drive is configured as the slave drive by using small jumpers on the drive body.

- Check all cable and power connections if the drive has occasional errors.

- Run programs like Disk Cleanup and Disk Defragmenter in the System Tools in the Accessories group of programs to repair common problems.

- Shut down the machine properly to avoid hard disk and data storage problems.

- Never move a computer while the hard disk is in operation. Shut down and turn off a computer before moving it.

- Check that the CMOS is correctly identifying the hard disk if the computer has trouble booting or produces hard disk-related error messages.

- Data can be recovered after most hard disk failures if critical information must be retrieved, but it is much more cost effective to make backups before a disaster occurs.

- Defective hard disks are replaced, not repaired. Opening a hard disk almost guarantees that it will need to be replaced.

Understanding file system characteristics

Windows operating systems have three formats for storing data on floppy and hard drives, as shown in **Table 2.9**. Domains, which are mentioned in the table, are a group of computers that are part of a network and share a common directory database.

Configuring IDE devices

Data transfers between Integrated Drive Electronics (IDE) devices and main memory occur using either of two modes:

Table 2.9: File system specifications

Specification	NTSF	FAT	FAT32
Compatible operating systems	Windows NT, Windows 2000, Windows XP	DOS, Windows 3.1, Windows 95, Windows 98, Windows Me, Windows NT, Windows 2000, Windows XP	Windows 95, OSR2, Windows 98, Windows Me, Windows 2000, Windows XP
Maximum file size	Limited only by size of volume	2 GB	Maximum file size 4 GB
Volume size range	Recommended from 10 MB to 2 TB; no floppy disks	Floppy disk size up to 4 GB.	512 MB to 2 TB; Windows 2000 limited to 32 GB
Domains	Supports domains	Does not support domains	Does not support domains

Programmed Input/Output (PIO) mode or Direct Memory Access (DMA) mode. In PIO mode, the CPU controls data transfers; in DMA mode, the device communicates directly with main memory. Advanced Technology Attachment (ATA) is the specification for a particular IDE interface. **Table 2.10** lists the standard PIO modes, while **Table 2.11** lists the standard DMA modes.

Table 2.10: *ATA PIO modes*

PIO mode	Data transfer rate	ATA revision
PIO-0	3.3 MBps	ATA
PIO-1	5.2 MBps	ATA
PIO-2	8.3 MBps	ATA
PIO-3	11.1 MBps	ATA-2
PIO-4	13.3 MBps	ATA-2
PIO-5	22.2 MBps	Never implemented

Table 2.11: *ATA DMA modes*

	DMA mode	Data transfer rate	ATA revision
Single Word modes	SDMA-0	2.1 MBps	ATA
	SDMA-1	4.2 MBps	ATA
	SDMA-2	8.3 MBps	ATA
Multiword modes	MDMA-0	4.2 MBps	ATA
	MDMA-1	13.3 MBps	ATA-2
	MDMA-2	16.6 MBps	ATA-2
Ultra DMA modes	UDMA-0	16.6 MBps	ATA-4
	UDMA-1	25.0 MBps	ATA-4
	UDMA-2	33.3 MBps	ATA-4
	UDMA-3	44.4 MBps	ATA-5
	UDMA-4	66.7 MBps	ATA-5
	UDMA-5	100.0 MBps	ATA-6
	UDMA-6	133.3 MBps	ATA-6/7

Modern PCs have two onboard IDE controllers. When you're installing IDE devices, keep the following guidelines in mind:

- Each IDE channel supports a maximum of two devices.

- If you're installing only one device on the bus, configure it as Single, Master, or Cable Select per the manufacturer's documentation.

- If you're installing two devices on the same bus, configure one as Master and the other as Slave, or both as Cable Select.

- In order to use the Cable-Select setting, the device, the ATA interface, and the interface cable must all support it.

- Always align Pin 1 on the interface cable (indicated by a colored stripe) with Pin 1 on the interface connector (indicated on the drive's circuit board or its chassis).

- Use 80-wire/40-socket interface cables on all devices, regardless of their ATA revision.

- UDMA cable connectors are color-coded. Attach the blue connector to the system board, the black connector to the master device, and the gray connector to the slave device.

- On a shared bus, each device operates at the speed of the slowest device. So, always install devices with similar data transfer rates on the same bus.

- Devices on the same bus can't perform simultaneous reads and writes. To optimize performance, install each device on its on channel whenever possible.

- Run your system's BIOS setup utility and configure your CMOS to Auto-Detect devices. If the device you're installing doesn't appear, you many need to upgrade your BIOS.

Working with floppy disk drives

Floppy disks, like those listed in **Table 2.12**, come in a variety of capacities. Current 3½" disk drives handle both 720 KB and 1.44 MB capacity disks. Windows XP can format DSHD (1.44 MB) floppy disks only, and floppy drives are not standard on some new computers.

Failure to read the contents of a floppy disk can indicate a problem with the disk or with the disk drive itself. The error message reported on the screen can help isolate the problem:

- Non-System Disk or Disk Error messages appear when you leave a floppy disk in the drive and attempt to boot up your machine. Remove the disk and press any key to continue.

- *The disk in drive A is not formatted* means the disk is not formatted or does not have a recognized format. Mac disks in an IBM machine cause this message. If you know the disk has no valuable data on it, format it.

Table 2.12: *Floppy disk characteristics*

Size	Type	Tracks per inch	Tracks per side	Sectors per track	Storage
3½"	DSDD	135	80	9	720 kB
3½"	DSHD	135	80	18	1.44 MB
3½"	DSED	135	80	36	2.88 MB

- *The disk is write-protected* means the write-protect tab is up and you can see through the write protect hole. Move the tab down to save information on the disk.

- Test the disk in another drive if it fails to be read on a suspect drive. If other drives can read the disk, replace the floppy drive. Replacement is more cost effective than repair.

- Don't test a series of disks on a suspect drive because the drive may be actively damaging the disks.

- Recover irreplaceable data on a bad disk using data recovery programs or services. Bad disks should be disposed of immediately so they are not unintentionally reused.

- Check the floppy drive controller setting in the CMOS and the Device Manager to make sure the settings are correct for 3 ½" 1.44 MB drives. Disable the built-in floppy controller on the motherboard and install an adapter card if the integrated floppy controller is proven to be defective.

- Examine the ribbon cable and ensure that it is securely attached at both ends with the correct orientation.

Working with optical media drives

CD-ROM and DVD disks have the same physical appearance, but DVD disks can store up to 17 GB of data in the double-layer, double-sided format. Keep the disks clean and the drives dust-free to avoid reading errors. Update drivers and secure all connections to fix most problems.

- Use CD-R disks for write once recording, and use CD-RW disks for multiple writes on the same disk.

- Replace older CD drives that are not designed to read CD-RW disks.

- Select Universal Disk Format (UDF) when creating a CD-ROM unless a situation requires ISO9660 or Joliet file formats.

- Reduce the drive speed if buffer under run errors occur during CD writing.

- Select from DVD-R or DVD+R, two distinct DVD formats, so the recorded DVD can be played on the target device. Some devices play only one of the formats.

- Insert a straightened paper clip into the small hole in the front of the drive to release the catch on the drive so that you can remove a stuck disk.

- Avoid paper labels, specifically asymmetrical labels, on CDs used in high speed drives.

- Allow high-speed CD writers to cool down between writing disks to avoid writing errors.

- Set the CD player to master or slave, depending on your setup. Use cable select if the cable connections are marked as master and slave.

- Adjust the BIOS settings if CD-ROM boot disks are not recognized.

Troubleshooting external peripherals
Many peripherals attach to the computer through external connectors or ports. Each port has specific characteristics that make it suitable for certain devices.

Configuring serial ports

A typical PC has at least one serial port, often labeled COM 1. Older systems used a 25-pin male connector, while newer systems and notebook computers use a 9-pin male connector. In order for two serial devices to communicate, they must have the same serial port settings. To change the port settings, which are listed in **Table 2.13**, open the property sheet for the port using Device Manager.

- Data Terminal Equipment (DTE) serial devices include computers, printers, and plotters, while Data Carrier Equipment (DCE) devices include modems, mice, and scanners. A DTE-DTE connection requires a different cable from DTE-DCE, so check the cable style if problems occur.

- Insert a null modem between standard serial cables to allow two computers to communicate through their serial ports. A null modem ensures the data send and receive wires are in the right places for both computers.

- Set the serial port settings in the Device Manager so the computer serial port is compatible with the peripheral device.

Table 2.13: *Serial port settings*

Setting	Description
Bits per second (bps)	Maximum communication speed at which data will pass through the port
Data bits	How many data bits are used for each character that is exchanged
Parity	The error-checking method
Stop bits	The time (in bits per second) between the transmission of each character that is sent
Flow control	How the flow of data is controlled and acknowledged

- Confirm there are no interrupt conflicts or I/O memory conflicts with other devices if a serial device fails or is unreliable.

Working with modems

The most common serial device connected to a computer is a modem, which also connects to your telephone service using an RJ-11 connector. Modems use standards developed by the International Telecommunications Union (ITU) and the Microcom Network Protocol (MNP) to implement data compression and error detection. **Table 2.14** lists the ITU standards and **Table 2.15** lists the MNP standards.

Most modems use the AT command set introduced by Hayes. The commands listed in **Table 2.16** are commands you can use with terminal software to control a modem.

The modem is just one of many potential sources of problems when your computer fails to communicate with the outside world. Experienced modem users can sometimes identify problems by listening for the hissing sounds generated by modems during the handshake process.

Table 2.14: *ITU standards*

Standard	Bits per second (bps)
V.32	9,600 bps; synchronous to 9,600; asynchronous is 4,800 bps
V.32 bis	14,400 bps (14.4 K bps); synchronous and asynchronous
V.34	28,800 bps (28.8 K bps)
V.34 bis	33,600 bps (33.6 K bps)
V.42	57,600 bps; specifies standards for error-checking
V.42 bis	56 Kbps receiving, 33.6 Kbps sending; specifies standards for compression
V.90	56 Kbps receiving, 33.6 Kbps sending; specifies standards for compression

- Check that your modem is compatible with your computer hardware and operating system, and replace it if it is not.

Table 2.15: *MNP standards*

Class	Description
1	The ability to send data in one direction at a time. This is referred to as *half-duplex*.
2	The ability to send and receive data simultaneously. This is referred to as *full-duplex*.
3	Improved throughput by having the sender strip start and stop bits prior to sending data and having the receiver add them back in.
4	Increased error correction through adjustable block sizes for the data based on the quality of the phone lines so that there is less need for retransmission of blocks of data.
5	Data compression to increase throughput. Redundant data is recoded by the sending modem into fewer bits to increase throughput. Data is uncompressed by the receiving modem prior to handing the data over to the receiving computer.

Table 2.16: *AT command set*

Command	Description
AT	Attention—used at the start of modem command lines
ATDT	Dial using touchtone
ATH	Hang up or disconnect
ATA	Answer
ATP	Dial using pulse (rotary dial)
,	Pause (each comma is roughly 3 seconds by default)
*70	Disable call waiting
Z	Reset
A/	Repeat—repeats the last command; often used to redial
+++	Escape character sequence—returns you to the command mode
0	Online—often used after the escape character sequence to continue communication

- Secure all cables and connectors and check for damaged wires.

- Place an outgoing call using a regular phone to make sure the phone line is working.

- Check the phone number for accuracy if the modem seems to work, but is unable to reach the desired location.

- Check the username and password if the modem seems to reach the desired location, but you aren't able to sign on.

- Switch modems if the current modem is not compatible with the destination modem.

- Redial at a later time if you can find no trouble spots at your machine. Some problems, such as down phone lines, phones that really are busy, defective modems on the other end of the line, and poor phone connections are out of your control.

Working with SCSI devices
SCSI devices are typically found on high-end workstations and servers, but you can also install them on standard desktop PCs. When you're installing SCSI devices, keep the following guidelines in mind:

- Depending on the SCSI implementation, you can connect either 8 or 16 devices to a single SCSI channel.

- Each device on a SCSI bus must have a unique SCSI ID.

- Depending on the SCSI implementation, you terminate either the device itself or the interface cable.

- If you're installing only internal devices, terminate the host adapter and the last internal device.

- If you're installing only external devices, terminate the host adapter and the last external device.

- If you're installing both internal and external devices, terminate the last internal device and the last external device, but remove the termination from the host adapter.

- Install only narrow devices on narrow busses and only wide devices on wide busses; otherwise, throughput is limited to the slowest device.

SCSI devices are often described in terms of the SCSI standards listed in **Table 2.17**. Within each standard, however, there are several SCSI implementations, which are listed in **Table 2.18** on the next page.

There are three different types of SCSI devices you can install: single-ended (SE) devices, low-voltage differential (LVD) devices, and high-voltage differential (HVD) devices. As shown in **Table 2.18**, the devices you can connect depend on the SCSI implementation.

Table 2.17: *SCSI standards*

SCSI type	Bus width	Throughput
SCSI-1	8 bits only	5 MBps
SCSI-2	8 bits only	10 MBps
SCSI-3	8 bits and 16 bits	20 MBps, 40 MBps, 80 MBps
SCSI-3	16 bits only	160 MBps, 320 MBps

Configuring parallel ports

The IEEE 1284 standard describes the bi-directional communication between the computer and peripherals over a parallel port connection. It identifies three different types of connectors: 1284 Type A, 1284 Type B, and 1284 Type C. As shown in **Table 2.19**, parallel ports can support either unidirectional or bi-directional data transfers. The port setting must match the requirements of the device attached to the port.

- Avoid daisy-chaining parallel port devices. If USB and FireWire connections are not an option, install separate parallel port adapter cards for extra parallel port devices.

Table 2.18: *SCSI implementations and their respective devices*

SCSI implementation	Clock rate	Bus width	Data transfer rate	
(Narrow) SCSI	5 MHz	8-bit	5 MBps	
Fast (Narrow) SCSI	10 MHz	8-bit	10 MBps	
Fast Wide SCSI	10 MHz	16-bit	20 MBps	
(Narrow) Ultra SCSI	20 MHz	8-bit	20 MBps	
(Narrow) Ultra SCSI	20 MHz	8-bit	20 MBps	
Wide Ultra SCSI	20 MHz	16-bit	40 MBps	
Wide Ultra SCSI	20 MHz	16-bit	40 MBps	
Wide Ultra SCSI	20 MHz	16-bit	40 MBps	
(Narrow) Ultra2 SCSI	40 MHz	8-bit	40 MBps	
Wide Ultra2 SCSI	40 MHz	16-bit	80 MBps	
Ultra3 SCSI (Ultra 160)	80 MHz	16-bit	160 MBps	
Ultra320 SCSI	160 MHz	16-bit	320 MBps	

- Select the proper settings for the parallel port and its associated peripheral in the CMOS if a device seems slow or unreliable. Options include output only, ECP, and bidirectional.

Table 2.19: *Types of parallel ports*

Type	Standard	Description	Typical devices
Unidirectional	SPP	Standard Parallel Port	Legacy printers
Bidirectional	ECP	Extended Capability Port	Modern printers and scanners
Bidirectional	EPP	Enhanced Parallel Port	Non-print devices, such as external drives and scanners

Maximum bus length for single-ended devices	Maximum bus length for LVD devices	Maximum bus length for HVD devices	Maximum number of devices
6 m	N/A	25 m	8
3 m	N/A	25 m	8
3 m	N/A	25 m	16
1.5 m	N/A	25 m	8
3 m	N/A	N/A	4
N/A	N/A	25 m	16
1.5 m	N/A	N/A	8
3 m	N/A	N/A	4
N/A	12 m	25 m	8
N/A	12 m	25 m	16
N/A	12 m	N/A	16
N/A	12 m	N/A	16

- Use high-quality IEEE-1284 cables to maintain reliable connections over longer distances.

Maintaining printers

Printers are often connected to the computer through the parallel port or LPT1. Most printers have a self-test option that prints a page without any computer input. If the self-test page fails to print, the problem is in the printer. If the self-test page prints correctly, the problem is in the computer or the cables.

- Printer quality is partly determined by pages per minute (PPM) and dots per inch (DPI) of the output. Printing technologies also determine quality.

- Update or reinstall the correct printer driver if no application can print.

- Adjust the Page Setup configuration in the application so the page prints the way the user expects.

- Install more memory in the printer if garbage characters appear.

- Troubleshoot network connections if a network printer fails to print for just a specific computer.

- Use paper designed for the printer, and adjust the printer so its output matches the thickness and quality of the paper being used.

- Repair or replace the fuser unit in a laser printer if the output is smeared or rubs off the paper.

- Check the rollers, corona wire, and the drum in laser printers if the quality of the output is low.

- Replace the inkjet cartridges if output quality is low. Remember to remove the tape that protects the head.

- Replace the inkjet printer for most other problems. Inkjet printer repair is not cost-effective.

- Replace the ribbon and align it correctly to correct most problems with dot matrix impact printers.

- Clean the print head or replace it if horizontal lines appear in the output of a dot matrix printer. Print head repair is not cost-effective.

Working with PS/2 devices

PS/2 ports were designed specifically for connecting a keyboard and a mouse to a computer system. The connectors look identical, but they aren't interchangeable. In most cases, you can identify the appropriate port by an icon imprinted on the I/O shield. On some systems, the mouse port is colored red, whereas the keyboard port is colored blue. PS/2 devices may not be unplugged and plugged in again successfully while Windows is up and running.

Standard keyboards are PS/2 devices, but USB, wireless, and infrared keyboards are also available. Keyboards generally have 101 keys, but special Windows keyboards have three additional keys. Some keyboards have buttons across the top of the keyboard to help automate common actions, such as sending email or signing on to the Internet.

- Replace a keyboard rather than repair it if the suggestions below don't solve the problem.

- Shake, brush, vacuum, or blow debris away from sticking keys.

- Accessibility options in the Control Panel may make the keyboard accessible to users with special needs, and they may also make the computer behave in ways that frustrate unsuspecting users.

- Check all cable connections and locations if the keyboard doesn't send information to the computer.

- Check the Control Panel settings for the keyboard if unexpected characters appear. An incorrect language or keyboard layout may be selected.

Table 2.20: *Keyboard shortcuts*

Key combination	Function
[WinKey]	Displays Taskbar and Start Menu
[F1]	Displays application help screen
[WinKey][F1]	Displays Windows help screen
[WinKey]E	Displays My Computer
[WinKey]F	Displays Find
[WinKey]R	Displays Run
[WinKey]D	Maximizes/Minimizes all windows
[WinKey]M	Minimizes all windows
[WinKey][Tab]	Moves between open applications in the taskbar
[WinKey][Ctrl]F	Finds a computer
[WinKey][Break]	Displays System Properties sheet
[Shift][Alt] [spacebar]	Opens Title Bar menu; use the arrow keys to navigate
[Alt]letter	Opens application menu with underlined letter
Letter	Goes to option with underlined letter in an open menu
[Enter]	Executes or activates the current selection

- Adjust the Control Panel settings for the proper delay before repeating when a key is held down, the rate of repeating, the function of the multimedia buttons, and other keyboard functions.

A defective mouse forces keyboard-only input. The keyboard shortcuts in **Table 2.20** simplify common activities used during computer diagnostics.

A mouse is a pointing device that controls the location of the cursor on the video screen. A mechanical mouse uses a rubber ball rolling on a mouse pad to turn wheels inside the mouse that send electrical impulses to the computer. An optical mouse uses light reflected from a mouse pad to control the cursor. A mouse may send information to the computer through wires, over infrared light, or by radio waves.

- Similar pointing devices are the TrackBall, TrackPoint, Touchpad, and joystick.

- Secure all cables in the correct ports if a mouse stops working, and then reboot the computer.

- Adjust the Control Panel settings so the buttons, scrolling wheel, and rate of motion are what the user expects.

- Update the mouse drivers if a mouse stops working when new software is added or the operating system is updated.

- Clean the mouse so the wheel makes good contact with the rollers, or the light and the receptor are clear.

- Replace the batteries and remove any obstructions if a cordless mouse malfunctions.

• Move a USB mouse to a powered hub or a computer port if it doesn't operate correctly from an unpowered hub.

Working with video displays

Computer displays, usually called monitors, are available in two varieties: Cathode Ray Tubes (CRT) and Liquid Crystal Displays (LCD). Some displays require analog connections, others require digital connections, and some support both analog and digital connections, as shown in **Table 2.21**.

• LCD screens are sometimes called *flat-panel*.

• CRTs are often a foot or more deep, and they may have a flat screen rather than a slightly curved screen.

• The quality of a monitor is determined by the screen size (check actual viewing area), the dot pitch (0.28 or smaller), the resolution (as large as affordable), and the refresh rate.

After you connect a display, you should configure its screen resolution and color depth. **Table 2.22** lists common screen resolutions and the amount of video RAM (number in parentheses) required to support various color depths.

Table 2.21: *Video cable and video card matches*

	DVI-D port	DVI-I port	DFP port	VGA port
DVI-D plug	Connects	Connects	Adapter	No
DVI-I plug	Adapter	Connects	Adapter	Adapter
DFP plug	Adapter	Adapter	Connects	No
VGA plug	No	Adapter	No	Connects
	Digital only	Analog/ digital	Digital only	Analog only

- Install screen savers for entertainment and privacy and adjust the timing to match the user's behavior. They are no longer needed to prevent screen burn-in.

- Change the settings for the Display Power Management System (DPMS) and Advanced Power Management (APM) settings in the Display control panel and the CMOS so power saving options don't interfere with the user's work schedule.

- Replace the video graphics card with one with more graphics memory and faster coprocessors if animation or game rendering is inadequate.

- Trace the power from the wall socket to the monitor if the monitor does not turn on.

- Adjust the contrast and brightness to the middle settings if no image appears on the screen.

- Secure all connections between the computer and the monitor.

- Replace the cable if there are broken or missing pins.

- Boot up in DOS and run Setup.exe in Win3.X systems if you can't see in Windows to change monitor settings.

Table 2.22: *Memory requirements for common resolutions and color depths*

Screen resolution	256 colors (8-bit)	Thousands of colors (16-bit)	Millions of colors (24-bit)
640 x 480	0.29 MB (512 KB)	0.59 MB (1 MB)	0.88 MB (1 MB)
800 x 600	0.46 MB (512 KB)	0.92 MB (1 MB)	1.37 MB (2 MB)
1024 x 768	0.75 MB (1 MB)	1.50 MB (2 MB)	2.25 MB (4 MB)
1280 x 1024	1.25 MB (2 MB)	2.50 MB (4 MB)	3.75 MB (4 MB)
1600 x 1200	1.83 MB (2 MB)	3.66 MB (4 MB)	5.49 MB (6 MB)

- Run Safe Mode in later Windows systems to boot up in VGA display mode so you can reinstall drivers or change monitor settings.

- Set screen resolution, color depth, and other video settings in the Display control panel. If a monitor squeals or make odd noises, change the monitor settings until the noise stops.

- Install the proper video drivers to display Motion Pictures Expert Group (MPEG), Audio Video Interleave (AVI), QuickTime, and Real video motion pictures correctly.

- Clean the touch screen, recalibrate the settings, and check all the connections if a touch screen has problems.

Working with sound devices

PCs support sound devices via either an onboard controller or an add-in card. **Table 2.23** lists the connectors found on sound cards.

- Insert microphones into Mic In and output from other audio devices into Line In to record sound with the appropriate amplification.

- Connect amplified speakers to Line Out for higher quality sound.

Table 2.23: *Connectors for sound and game devices*

Port or interface	Description
Mic In	Microphone input
Speaker Out	Output to stand-alone speakers
Line Out	Output to speakers with amplifiers
Line In	Input from other amplifier
Game Port	Input from joystick or game controller
Midi Port	Connection to electronic musical instrument

A+ Certification Troubleshooting and Repair Pocket Guide

- Attach unamplified speakers to Speaker Out for lower quality sound.

- Use the Musical Instrument Digital Interface (MIDI) port to interact with compatible electronic musical instruments.

- Configure sound settings in Start | Programs | Accessories | Entertainment | Volume Control for desired sound quality and volume levels.

- Configure the Game/Midi port to match the required settings for joysticks and other game control panels.

- Install quality jacks and shielded cables for better quality sound.

Installing and configuring USB devices

USB is a serial bus technology that supports up to 127 devices in a hierarchical topology. USB and FireWire are taking the place of serial and parallel connections for most peripherals. The USB host controller serves as the root of the hierarchy, and devices, such as hubs and bridges, allow you to extend the topology. **Table 2.24** lists the USB standards in use today.

Table 2.24: *USB characteristics*

Industry name	Maximum data rate	Typical devices
Low Speed USB 1.0	1.5 Mbps	Keyboard, mouse, stylus, game peripherals, virtual reality peripherals
Full Speed USB 1.1	12 Mbps	Telephone service, broadband service, audio, microphone
High Speed USB 2	480 Mbps	Video, storage, imaging, broadband

USB cables use a Type A connector for the upstream connection and a Type B connector for the downstream connection. Consumer electronic devices, such as cameras, typically use a mini-A/B connector.

- Enable USB support on your system if USB ports and hubs refuse to work. Older computers may need upgraded software and hardware (PCI to USB adapter card, for example) to support USB. Windows 95 OSR 2.1 and later can support USB with compatible hardware and drivers.

- Try the device on another USB compatible computer if it is not recognized or fails to work on the first computer. Replace the device if it is defective. If it works correctly on another computer, and other USB devices work on the first computer, reinstall the USB drivers and the device drivers on the first computer.

- Replace the USB hub or reinstall the USB drivers if all USB devices fail to work on a computer.

Installing and configuring FireWire devices
FireWire is a serial bus technology that supports up to 64 devices in a serial topology. You can extend the topology using hubs and bridges. FireWire is Apple's name for the technology and iLink is Sony's name. **Table 2.25** lists the FireWire standards in use today.

Table 2.25: *Connectors for sound and game devices*

Industry name	Maximum data rate	Typical devices
IEEE 1394A (FireWire 400)	100, 200, and 400 Mbps	Hard drives, scanners, printers, CD-RWs
IEEE 1394B (FireWire 800)	800 Mbps	Digital video camcorders

Table 2.26: *Battery types used in portable devices*

Battery type	Description
Nickel Cadmium (NiCad)	The battery type used in the original portable computers. Heaviest and least expensive. Short life of three to four hours. Recharge can take up to 12 hours. Can be recharged approximately 700 to 1,000 times. Remembers how full it was when last recharged and doesn't go past that point the next time it is charged. This is referred to as the memory effect.
Nickel Metal-Hydride (NiMH)	Environmentally friendly because it doesn't contain heavy metals that can be toxic. Uses nickel and metal hydride plates with potassium hydroxide as the electrolyte. Uses a liquid electrolyte which must be contained in protective steel cans to prevent leakage. Doesn't hold charges as well as NiCad when not in use, but provides up to 50 percent more power than NiCad for the same weight. Doesn't suffer from memory effect. More expensive than NiCad. Can be recharged approximately 400 to 500 times.
Li-Ion	Lithium based. A lightweight metal. Provides light, long-life battery. Holds a charge well. Can't be overcharged. Holds twice as much power as NiCad. Weighs about half as much as NiCad. Provides higher power than NiCad. More expensive than NiCad. Can be recharged approximately 400 to 500 times. Uses a liquid electrolyte which must be contained in protective steel cans to prevent leakage.
Lithium Polymer	Similar to Li-Ion in power. Uses a jelly-like material as an electrolyte instead of liquid. This enables power cells to be manufactured in various shapes and sizes for custom requirements.
Zinc Air	Provides more charge per pound than NiCad or NiMH. Doesn't suffer from the memory effect. Uses a carbon membrane that absorbs oxygen, a zinc plate, and potassium hydroxide as the electrolyte.

FireWire 400 uses 4-pin connectors on notebook computers and consumer electronics devices and a 6-pin connector on desktop systems. FireWire 800 uses a 9-pin cable on both types of systems. To interconnect FireWire 400 and FireWire 800 devices, you need to use a cable that supports bilingual communications.

Working with portable computing devices

Portable computers often have the power of a desktop compressed into a much smaller container. While most of the techniques for maintaining and configuring desktop computers also apply to portable computers, mobile computing devices have some special needs.

Portable devices depend on batteries for power, even though many can also be powered by wall adapters. Batteries come in a variety of styles and prices, but most devices require very specific types of batteries. **Table 2.26** on the previous page compares the batteries commonly used in portable devices.

Three types of PC cards are commonly in use with portable computers. **Table 2.27** lists the three types of memory cards commonly in use with portable devices.

Table 2.27: *PC card types*

Type	Thickness	Used primarily for
I	3.3 mm	Memory
II	5.0 mm	Memory, modems, network adapters, wireless network adapters, USB, FireWire, and SCSI connectors; might have pop-out connectors for network cables or phone line connections
III	10.5 mm	Miniature hard drives

Table 2.28: *Memory options for portable devices*

Name	Physical size	Capacity	Description
CompactFlash	43 mm long x 36 mm wide. Type I is 3.3 mm thick and Type II is 5 mm thick.	8 MB to 1 GB	Composed of memory chips and a controller. Has a 50-pin contact.
SmartMedia	45 mm long x 37 mm wide x 0.76 mm thick. Weighs 1.8 grams.	2, 4, 8, 16, 32, 64, or 128 MB	Contains only a memory chip and no controller. Controller is in the device that the card is inserted into. Older cards ran at 5 V and have the notch on the left. Newer cards run at 3.3 V and have the notch on the right.
xD-Picture Card (xD)	20 mm long x 25 mm wide x 1.7 mm thick. Weighs 2 grams.	16 MB to 256 MB with plans for up to 8 GB	Contains only a memory chip and no controller. Controller is in the device that the card is inserted into. Half the size of SmartMedia cards.
Memory Stick (MS)	50 mm long x 21.5 mm wide x 2.8 mm thick. Weighs 4 grams.	4, 8, 16, 32, 64, and 128 MB	Used extensively in Sony products. Memory Stick Pro is one-half the size of a MS card and is 1 GB.
Secure Digital (SD) and MultiMedia Card (MMC)	32 mm long x 24 mm wide x 2.1 mm thick.	4 to 512 MB	Composed of memory chip(s), controller module, and copper balls between chips. SD and MMC are the same physically, but technically they are different. Some systems can only use SD. A new variety, SD-I/O with built-in Bluetooth technology for wireless transfer of data. There are also SD Audio and SD Memory Cards.

Portable devices use a variety of memory. Some memory is designed to be used in the device, such as a camera, and then removed and inserted in a second device so data can be transferred. **Table 2.28** on the previous page lists common memory options.

Batteries cause the most problems for portable devices. Check the batteries for full charges and secure connections first before attempting other repairs.

- Use the correct keyboard combination to switch between internal and external monitors if a display is incorrect.

- Maintain proper ventilation and add cooling options if the device overheats.

- Reset power-saving options so the timing of hibernation and power-downs match the user's work schedule.

- Secure all dock station connections and memory card connections if the device does not work as expected.

- Recharge other batteries to make sure the battery charger is effective.

Section III: Supporting Computer Operating Systems

Without an operating system and applications, a computer is just hardware, not a useful tool. Choosing the right system software and applications determines the value of the computer in a work environment. The vast majority of business and home computers use Microsoft Windows and compatible applications. This section will help you support and upgrade these systems.

Identifying software classifications

Software provides the interface between the user, the applications, the operating system, and the hardware. As described below, there are several different types of software, each serving a special purpose:

- **System software.** The operating system, compilers, loaders, and utility programs make up the system software. The system software manages all the other programs on the computer. Popular microcomputer system software includes Windows, UNIX, and the Macintosh operating system.

- **Application software.** A program that performs a specific function for the user is application software. Examples of application software are word processors, database managers, spreadsheets, and graphics programs. Applications require specific system software and hardware configurations to function.

- **Driver software.** Programs that interact with a particular computer device are drivers. Drivers contain very specific information that must be available so a computer can communicate with individual peripherals. For example, application software generates general print commands.

The printer driver translates these commands into specific instructions required by the make and model of the printer that is attached to the computer.

- **Firmware.** Computer programs or data that are written onto ROM memory are firmware. Firmware is permanent software that is often used to run printers, modems and other computer devices. Microcode is another name for firmware. The BIOS (Basic Input Output System) is firmware found on all personal computers.

Troubleshooting the boot process

The most serious computer disasters appear during the boot up process. Several options are available to you during this process that help you isolate and fix the problems.

Inside the Power-On Self-Test (POST)

When the computer is first turned on, the ROM BIOS firmware performs a series of tests called the Power-On

Table 3.1: *Common error codes for different makes of BIOS*

Beeps	IBM	AMI	Phoenix
None	Power supply defective, speaker problem, or major motherboard problem		
Continuous	Power supply, system board, or keyboard problem		
One	Normal POST—system is okay	Normal POST—system is okay	When followed by other beeps, motherboard is bad
Two short	POST Error—error code shown on the screen	Memory problems—error code shown on the screen	When followed by other beeps, memory is bad

Self-Test (POST). The BIOS uses configuration information stored in the CMOS to ensure the computer hardware is working. A pattern of beeps or displayed error codes usually indicates a chip is loose on the motherboard, or the motherboard is faulty. If the error code is not listed in **Table 3.1**, look up the meaning of the code in a resource manual for that make and model BIOS.

- Upgrade your BIOS when you want to add new hardware that is not recognized by your current BIOS. Some BIOS are burned into ROM chips, and the entire chip must be replaced. Flash memory BIOS can be upgraded using special software from the manufacturer.

- Treat the BIOS carefully because your entire computer depends on it. Make sure any changes conform to all the computer specifications and requirements.

- Open the CMOS setup screen by pressing the key displayed on the opening screen—usually [F1], [F2], or [Delete].

- Enter a password, if required, to edit CMOS data. If you don't know the password, consult the user manual for a bypass. If required, you can disconnect the CMOS battery so it forgets a password is required. You'll have to completely reconfigure the CMOS, but you will have access to it.

- Display Startup Options by pressing [F8] during the POST in Win 95 and XP. Press [Ctrl] in Win 95 to display the startup options.

- Press other keys for other options. HP offers a recovery mode during the POST. The HP recovery mode can destroy all data and user-installed programs and should be used only in the most extreme situations.

Configuring CMOS
CMOS settings control the basic hardware functions of the computer. Many hardware problems can be traced back to improper CMOS settings. The starting screen will tell you exactly what key to press to enter Set Up on a specific machine.

- Enable the Boot Time Diagnostic Screen to display the POST process and the basic hardware settings. If this screen is not enabled, certain problems may not be visible to the user.

- Write down all the settings, or use a utility that prints out the settings, so you are able to restore the CMOS settings to the current values.

- Replace the CMOS battery if the time, date, or other settings prove unreliable.

- Change the boot sequence if you need to boot from a CD-ROM instead of the floppy disk or hard disk.

- Ensure that all the IDE settings and other port settings are optimized for the specific devices attached to the computer.

Using Startup modes to help you diagnose problems
Startup options help you solve problems by restricting the software executed during the boot-up process. By adding additional software one program at a time, you can sometimes isolate the problem. Repeatedly tap [F8] during the POST to bring up the screen of options. Commonly used Windows XP options are as follows:

- Safe Mode uses the minimum amount of device drivers and services to start Windows.

- Safe Mode With Networking adds network drivers to the minimum set.

- Safe Mode With Command Prompt starts a text-based interface, Cmd.exe, instead of Windows Explorer. Type **help** to see a list of your options. In Windows XP, this is called the Recovery Console.

- Enable VGA Mode starts Windows in 640 x 480 mode. This is useful if current display settings don't work on the monitor, and you need to reset them.

- Last Known Good Configuration starts Windows by using a previous good configuration.

Working with DOS and the real-mode environment

MS-DOS (Microsoft Disk Operating System) is found on legacy systems and is the backbone of Win 3.x and Win 9x systems. MS-DOS boot floppy disks can be created to maintain

Table 3.2: *Order and function of DOS boot files*

Order	File	Function
1	IO.SYS	Interfaces the low-level hardware
2	MSDOS.SYS	Translate software commands into commands IO.SYS can execute
3	CONFIG.SYS	Activates or manages memory areas and device drivers
4	COMMAND.COM	Allows the user to communicate with MS-DOS
5	AUTOEXEC.BAT	Loads TSRs and configures the DOS environment
6	DBLSPACE.BIN	Allows access to compressed drives

and repair these operating systems. Once the system passes the POST, the DOS boot files in **Table 3.2** on the previous page will take control of the machine in DOS, Windows 3.x, and Windows 9x machines. Windows NT, Windows 2000, and Windows XP operating systems do not load DOS.

- Make backup copies of AUTOEXEC.BAT and CONFIG.SYS so you can restore working settings if new installations or drive errors corrupt these vital files.

- Replace damaged files and correct errors contained in the boot-up files if DOS fails during the boot-up process.

- System files are usually hidden. The first file is stored on a specific part of the boot disk and is useless if moved to another location.

Configuring DOS memory
Original IBM compatible machines were restricted to 1 MB of RAM. Later machines could handle more memory. **Table 3.3** indicates how that memory is allocated for DOS-based machines.

Without additional programming, a DOS machine uses conventional memory for programs, and reserve memory for hardware. The CONFIG.SYS program can execute soft-

Table 3.3: *DOS memory allocation*

Range	Name of memory	Typical use
0–640 KB	Conventional, lower, or base memory	Store DOS, device drivers, TSRs, and applications
640 KB–1 MB	Reserve or Upper Memory Area (UMA)	Store hardware information and BIOS programming information
1 MB+	Extended (XMS)	Holds data and code

ware that activates and manages other memory locations. These additional programs are required by Windows 3.x.

- HIMEM.SYS manages memory above 1 MB and makes this available to compatible DOS programs.

- EMM386.EXE simulates expanded memory (page swapping) in extended memory and provides access to the reserve memory.

- DOS=HIGH loads portions of DOS in the High Memory Area (HMA), the 64 KB just above the first 1 MB of RAM.

- DOS=UMB allows DOS to manage the Upper Memory Blocks (UMB) created by EMM386.EXE in the UMA.

Essential DOS commands

After DOS boots up, you can use line commands to control and analyze files on the machine. The commands that will execute depend on the files on the boot-up disk. **Table 3.4** lists useful commands and their syntax.

Table 3.4: *DOS commands*

Command	Function
ATTRIB	Shows all the files with their attributes
FORMAT A: /S	Makes a bootable disk containing required system files
CD\DOS	Changes the current directory to the DOS directory
DIR/P	Shows all the files, in the current directory, one screen at a time
EDIT CONFIG.SYS	Opens a text editor and displays CONFIG.SYS for editing
TREE /F |MORE	Shows a scrollable list of directories and files
TYPE AUTOEXEC.BAT	Displays content of AUTOEXEC.BAT

Windows 9x support for the real-mode environment

Windows 3.x is a Graphical User Interface (GUI) that is loaded after MS-DOS boots up in older computers. Later Windows versions, such as Windows 95/98/Me, continue to create similar support files for backward compatibility. To view available system support files in Windows XP, select Start | Run and enter sysedit. The support files listed in **Table 3.5** can be modified to control the Windows environment.

Creating DOS startup and emergency repair disks

Each operating system has a method for creating a start-up disk. A DOS startup disk will give you access to the files on your hard drive. DOS startup disks created in Windows XP contain just the files you need to reach the A:\> prompt, as shown in **Table 3.6**.

- In Windows XP, to create an MS-DOS boot disk, open My Computer, insert a floppy disk in Drive A, select Drive A:, choose File | Format, and select Create An MS-DOS Startup Disk.

- The MS-DOS boot disk created in XP contains no diagnostic or repair files.

Table 3.5: *Windows 3.X support files*

File Name	Description
WIN.INI	Controls the Windows environment
PROGRAM.INI	Controls the Program Manager
SYSTEM.INI	Customizes Windows to meet the system's hardware needs
WINFILE.INI	Controls the appearance and behavior of the File Manager
CONTROL.INI	Controls screen appearance, drivers, and some settings

- To learn more about the specific files, at the A prompt (A:\>) enter MODE.COM /?, for example. A help screen will appear if the program has one available.

- In Windows XP, you can boot up your machine using the installation CD-ROM for Windows XP and choose to repair the installation. The installation CD-ROM takes the place of Emergency Repair Disks (ERD) created in older operating systems.

- In Windows 2000, select Start | Programs | Accessories | System Tools | Backup | Tools | Create Emergency Repair Disk to create an ERD with a few tools to help you repair typical problems with your hard drive.

Table 3.6: *Files on a DOS startup disk created in Windows XP*

Files	Function
COMMAND.COM	Allows the user to communicate with MS-DOS
CONFIG.SYS	Activates or manages memory areas and device drivers
DISPLAY.SYS EGA2.CPI EGA3.CPI EGA.CPI	Enables the display of international character sets on EGA, VGA, and LCD monitors
IO.SYS	Interfaces the low-level hardware
KEY.COM KEYBOARD.SYS KEYBRD2.SYS KEYBRD3.SYS KEYBRD4.SYS	Configures the keyboard for a specific language
MODE.COM	Configures the system devices like COM ports and LPT ports
MSDOS.SYS	Translates software commands into commands IO.SYS can execute

- Recovery disks supplied by computer manufacturers restore the hard disk to the condition it was in when the computer was first delivered. That means all data and user-installed applications are destroyed. Recovery disks are the last resort. They only work on the make and model computer that they were shipped with.

- Programs like FORMAT.COM in Windows XP directory, Windows\System32, will not work under the DOS operating system and can't be copied to the disk.

- For a floppy boot disk to give you access to CD-ROM drives, you need drivers on the boot disk specific to the CD-ROM drives on the machine.

- Many Web sites offer files for boot-up disks with collections of analysis and repair files. Use only those files guaranteed compatible with the operating system and file structure or you can destroy data and files.

Working with Windows 9x/2000/XP and the protected-mode environment

Once a system completes its POST and the real-mode portion of the operating system completes, the protected-mode portion of the operating system finishes assigning system resources and brings the system to a fully operable state. In the sections that follow, we'll describe some tools you can use in this environment to help you maintain and troubleshoot a system.

Using Windows XP's System Restore utility

System Restore reconfigures the system to a previous state when problems occur with the EXE or DLL files or applications. Restore does not harm data files, emails, Internet histories, and similar files, and should be tried before other, riskier, methods are attempted. Restore tracks changes, including application installation and driver updates, and if an update or installation causes a problem, restore brings the system back to its condition before the installation or update.

- Right-click on My Computer and select System Properties | System Restore to make sure that important drives are currently being monitored and can be restored.

- If Windows XP does not start, press [F8] during the boot-up process and navigate with the arrow keys to Last Known Good Configuration and press the [Enter] key.

- If Windows XP starts, log on as the administrator, select Start | Programs | Accessories | System Tools | System Restore. Respond to the Restore Wizard so you can select the correct settings.

- Undo a restore operation by going to the Restore Wizard and selecting Undo my last restoration.

Using the Windows XP Recovery Console
If your Windows XP does not start properly, or doesn't even start at all, the Windows XP Recovery Console may be able to help you recover. The Recovery Module uses a text-based interface that lets the XP administrator modify a restricted set of files and folders with the following options:

- Use, copy, rename, or replace operating system files and folders.

- Enable or disable service or device startup when you next start your computer.

- Repair the file system boot sector or the Master Boot Record (MBR).

- Create and format partitions on drives.

Because many computers come with Windows XP installed, the user may not have setup floppy disks or the Windows CD-ROM available. Microsoft offers online versions of setup disks. The following methods will start up the Recovery Console:

- Start your computer by using the Windows Setup floppy disks or the Windows CD-ROM. At the Welcome To Setup screen, press [F10] or [R] to repair and start the Windows Recovery Console. Pressing [F10] may lead to a recovery process wizard created by the manufacturer rather than the Windows Recovery Console.

- Press [F8] during the boot-up process and select Safe Mode with Command Prompt to gain access to the Recovery Console.

- Add the Windows Recovery Console to the Windows Startup folder by using the Winnt32.exe utility with the /cmdcons option (D:\i386\winnt32.exe /cmdcons). This procedure requires approximately 7 MB of hard disk space on the system partition to hold the Cmdcons folder and files.

- Depending on your installation, System Properties | Advanced | Setup And Recovery may provide options for listing the Recovery Console as an optional operating system during boot-up.

- Type help at the console prompt to see the commands available on the Recovery Console.

Troubleshooting tools integrated into Windows 9x/2000/XP

A related set of support tools can be run from a command line in Windows. Choosing Start | Program | Accessories | Command Prompt opens the Command Line window. Type help for a complete list of available commands, some of which are shown in **Table 3.7** on the next page.

If the operating system comes up, you will have access to a wide variety of support files. Each version of Windows offers a specific set of support files in the System Tools area of the Accessories Program Group, as shown in **Table 3.8**, also on the next page. Rescue disks and Emergency Repair disks must have compatible files copied to the disk before you can perform the operations.

Understanding Windows upgrade and support options

Many hardware and software problems can be eliminated by upgrading to a later version of Windows. The following section discusses upgrade options.

Windows 9x (Win 95, Win 98, Win 98 SE, Win Me) are GUIs that have some level of dependence on DOS. Windows 95 is available with OEM Service Release 1 (OSR1) and OSR2, Windows 98 has its first and Second Edition (SE), and Windows Me is usually considered part of the Win 9x group.

- Compared to Win 3.x, Win 95 supplied a superior GUI, it multitasked better, it was more reliable, and ran 32-bit applications.

- Win 98 added a FAT16 to FAT32 conversion utility, multiple monitor support, and WebTV for Windows.

Table 3.7: *File system specifications*

Tool	Used to	
Defrag	Defragment hard drives.	
Set	Configure environment variables.	
Setver	Configure the version of DOS Windows reports to a program. Used to simulate an older version of DOS if an application won't run in Windows 2000/XP/NT.	
Ver	Display operating system version.	
chkdsk	Enable you to check the hard disk for errors. If any errors are reported, you can then use other tools, such as ScanDisk, to repair those errors.	
Fdisk	View, create, or delete partitions, and to mark a primary partition as active.	
Format	Format a disk. You can also use it to format a disk and make it bootable.	
Mem	View the memory usage on a computer, including the conventional, upper memory, and high memory area segments.	
Msd	View system information.	
Scandisk	Perform a thorough check of a hard disk and repair any errors it encounters.	

Table 3.8: *Windows-based support files*

Operating system	System Tools menu contents	
Windows 98	Backup, Disk Cleanup, Disk Defragmenter, Drive Converter, Maintenance Wizard, ScanDisk, Scheduled Tasks, System Information, and Welcome To Windows	
Windows 2000	Backup, Character Map, Disk Cleanup, Disk Defragmenter, Getting Started, Scheduled Tasks, and System Information	

Sample syntax	Supported operating systems
`defrag volume`	Windows 98 and Windows XP
`set variable=string`	Windows 98, Windows NT, Windows 2000, and Windows XP
`setver drive:path filename DOSversion`	Windows 98, Windows NT, Windows 2000, and Windows XP
`Ver`	Windows 98, Windows NT, Windows 2000, and Windows XP
Enter `chkdsk drive letter`. For example, to check the C drive, enter `chkdsk C:`.	DOS
	DOS
Enter `format A: /s` to format a floppy disk and make it bootable.	DOS
Enter `mem`.	DOS
Enter `msd` to start the Msd utility.	DOS
Enter `scandisk drive letter`.	DOS

Operating system	System Tools menu contents
Windows XP	Activate Windows, Backup, Character Map, Disk Cleanup, Disk Defragmenter, Files And Settings Transfer Wizard, Scheduled Tasks, System Information, and System Restore

- Windows Me added System Restore and Windows Critical Update Notification to a Windows 98 SE starting point, and offered features to help novice user work the OS.

There are several types of Windows servers, as described next:

- Windows NT Servers were a new operating system completely independent of MS-DOS, written to provide stability and security to networked systems.

- Windows 2000 is available as Windows 2000 Professional, Windows 2000 Server, Windows 2000 Advanced Server, and Windows 2000 Datacenter Server, each with special networking capabilities.

- The Windows XP family of operating systems is built on Windows 2000 server and is available in XP Home, XP Office, XP Media Center, XP Tablet PC, and XP 64-bit editions.

- Windows 2003 Server is available in the Standard Edition, Enterprise Edition, Datacenter Edition, and Web Edition—each with specifications designed for a particular function. It offers improved security, reliability, availability, and scalability, as well as Microsoft .NET for connecting information, people, systems, and devices.

Support from Microsoft should be a major consideration when deciding on an upgrade path. Microsoft offers no-charge incident support, paid incident support, support charged on an hourly basis, support for warranty claims, hotfix support, and online self-help support information from the date of introduction to the end of mainstream support. After mainstream support, Microsoft offers assisted support, which may be charged on an hourly basis and can include hotfix support until the extended phase ends. Microsoft will not accept requests for warranty support, design changes, or new features during the extended phase. The timeline information in **Table 3.9** can help determine the life remaining in Windows operating systems.

Inadequate hardware for the installed operating system causes many problems. If the hardware permits it, updating the system software often resolves trouble. **Table 3.10** on the next page lists the basic requirements for Windows operating systems.

Table 3.9: *Windows desktop support life-cycle summary*

OS version	Introduced	End of mainstream support	Current status
MS-DOS, Windows 3.x, Windows NT, Windows 95	NA	NA	No support
Win 98	Jun 30, 1998	Jun 30, 2002	Extended support to Jan 16, 2004
Win 98 Second Edition	Jun 30, 1999	Jun 30, 2002	Extended support to Jan 16, 2004
2000 Professional	Mar 31, 2000	Mar 31, 2005	Extended support to Mar 31, 2007
Millennium Edition	Dec 31, 2000	Dec 31, 2003	Extended support to Dec 31, 2004
XP Professional	Dec 31, 2001	Dec 31, 2006	Extended support to Dec 31, 2008
XP Home Edition	Dec 31, 2001	Dec 31, 2006	No extended support

When a customer suggests upgrading hardware or the operating system, the following considerations will help guide them to a rational decision.

- Advise upgrading if the computer is too slow, new software requires a new operating system, or new hardware is incompatible with the current system.

- Avoid upgrading components in an existing system when it is more cost effective to buy a completely new system.

- Right-click on My Computer and choose Properties to confirm the computer system has the hardware needed to run a new operating system.

- Run all system, driver, and application updates to confirm that the problems are permanent and that a major upgrade is needed.

Table 3.10: Minimum system requirements for Windows—recommended in parentheses

Component	Win 95	Win 98	Win Me	Win 2000	Win XP
Processor	386DX (486)	486DX 66 (Pentium)	Pentium 150-MHz	Pentium 133 MHz	Pentium 233 (300 MHz)
Memory	4 MB (8 MB)	16 MB (24 MB)	32 MB	64 MB	64 MB (128 MB)
Hard disk space	50-55 MB	120 MB to 355 MB	320 MB	2 GB	1.5 GB
Hardware	3.5" HD	3.5" HD	3.5" HD, CD-ROM, or DVD drive	CD-ROM or DVD drive	CD-ROM or DVD-ROM, sound card, speakers
Video	VGA (SVGA)	VGA (SVGA)	VGA or higher	VGA or higher	Super VGA (800 x 600)

Because Microsoft has stopped supporting earlier Windows versions, most users will want to upgrade to Windows XP. While any user can purchase the full version of Windows XP, users running specific previous versions of Windows can purchase a less expensive upgrade package. Only owners with the Windows versions shown in **Table 3.11** are eligible for upgrades.

Table 3.11: *Windows XP upgrades*

Previous version	Windows XP Home	Windows XP Professional
Windows 98/98SE	Yes	Yes
Windows Me	Yes	Yes
Windows NT 4.0	No	Yes
Windows 2000 Pro	No	Yes
Windows XP Home	-	Yes
Windows XP Pro	No	-

Table 3.12: *Windows XP Editions*

Version	Features
Home	Home edition provides more speed, security, connectivity, and reliability than Windows 98.
Professional	Designed for business use. Windows XP Home plus increased security, networking capabilities, remote access, and advanced features.
Media Center	Available only on PCs with required entertainment hardware from Microsoft's manufacturer partners. Windows XP Pro plus digital entertainment software and capabilities.
Tablet PC	Designed for Tablet PCs. Windows XP Pro plus handwriting and speech recognition capabilities.
64-bit Edition	Supports up to 16 GB of RAM and 16 TB of virtual memory. Designed to work on the Intel Itanium processor.

Several versions of Windows XP are available. **Table 3.12** on the previous page explains the major differences. Several CD-ROM versions are available for users who choose to upgrade. **Table 3.13** describes some of the versions available.

To install or update to Windows XP, you need to follow the directions as presented in the Install program. The following tips will help the process proceed successfully.

- Assure that the computer has the required components, that all important applications are compatible with Windows XP, the original installation programs for re-installing needed applications are available, and that all data is backed up and verified.

- Before starting installation, record the CD key, the Internet connection data from the ISP, and the network connection information.

- If updating, check that you have an upgradeable version of Windows on the master hard drive, or else have a CD containing an upgradeable version of Windows.

Table 3.13: *Windows XP installation disk formats*

Version	Features
Upgrade version	Will only upgrade certain versions of Windows. If a suitable version of Windows is not already installed, you need access to the original installation CD-ROM.
Full version	Will install Windows XP on a blank drive or a drive with an old system on it.
OEM version	Limited XP version sold with a computer. Will work only on that specific computer make and model.
Recovery version	Will return the hard drive to the condition at the time of sale. It may destroy all stored data.

- Each CD can install Windows XP on just one machine, so make sure no one else has used the CD on another machine.

- Insert the CD, choose upgrade, accept the License agreement, enter the product key, and confirm there are no major problems in the Upgrade Report.

- Wait to activate the copy of Windows XP if the user intends to upgrade the hardware in the near future.

- Follow the installation instructions and insert needed information when prompted.

Safeguarding your customers' data

Weekly and daily backups must always be made for all important data. Backup procedures range from copying files to floppy disks or CD-ROMs to automatic backup programs that allow you to select which files to back up and when they should be backed up. Windows XP Home Edition does not install a backup program by default, so users may need third-party programs.

- Windows XP Home Edition does not install the backup program. Double-click on ntbackup.msi in \VALUEADD\ MSFT\NTBACKUP on the Windows XP CD-ROM to install the backup program.

- Select Start | Programs | Accessories | System Tools | Backup to start the Backup Wizard if the Backup Program is installed in Windows XP.

- Tell the wizard what you want to back up, where you want the copies to be stored, and when you want to schedule automatic backups.

Understanding backup strategies

Backup programs offer different types of backup for your files, as shown in **Table 3.14**. Choosing the wrong backup method can miss saving needed files and save other unneeded files.

- Use several different sets of backup disks so you are not making another backup on top of your only good backup data.

- The frequency of backup sessions depends on how much data and effort the user is willing to lose. The time between backups may range from a day to a week, while copies of critical files may be made as soon as changes occur.

Protecting a system from viruses

Many computer problems can be traced back to malicious software, or malware, such as viruses and Trojan horses. Some users tend to blame every problem on viruses.

Table 3.15 lists the major classifications of malicious software and their impact on a computer system.

Table 3.14: *File system specifications*

Type	Description
Full	Back up all the selected files and turn off the archive file attribute.
Incremental	Back up selected files only if the archive attribute is set. Turn off archive attribute after backing up the file.
Differential	Back up selected files only if the archive attribute is set. Leave the archive attribute turned on.
Copy	Back up selected files, ignoring the archive attribute. The archive attribute is left unchanged.

Viruses can be divided in categories, depending on where and how they affect the computer. **Table 3.16** lists the major classifications of common viruses.

Avoiding malicious software requires a few simple procedures that must be followed consistently. Preventative measures are more cost-effective than virus removal. Symptoms of a virus infection include failure to boot up,

Table 3.15: *Malicious software*

Type	Function
Virus	Deliberately written computer code that replicates itself and spreads, often causing damage, without the user's knowledge or permission.
Worms	Viruses that send copies of themselves through emails or Internet Relay Chat.
Trojan horses	Programs that pretend to be a benign application but perform an unexpected and usually unwanted operation.
Logic bomb	A Trojan horse that executes only when a predetermined set of conditions exists on the computer.
Spyware	Programs that monitor computer usage and transmit data without the user's knowledge or permission.

Table 3.16: *Virus classifications*

Type	Function
Boot sector	Virus code that infects the boot sector or master boot program on the hard drive.
File	Virus code that attaches to or replaces executable files.
Macro	Virus code stored in a data document and spread when the document is opened. Macros can be transferred through emails.
Polymorphic	Virus code that changes its signature to prevent detection by an antivirus program.

unintentionally reformatted drives, corrupt files, or unexpected messages on the screen.

- Install and always use antivirus software that inspects all opened files, inserted disks, email downloads, and message attachments for known and possible viruses.

- Update your antivirus program weekly or use an automatic update subscription so you are protected against the latest malware.

- Never download files, open attachments, or run unknown software without scanning it for viruses.

- Update your operating system and browser programs to plug known security weaknesses.

- Scan all your files on a regular basis for viruses.

- Create emergency bootable disks that can execute virus scan software.

- Write-protect your floppies before inserting them into other computers.

Virus hoaxes are often email warnings of nonexistent viruses that tie up mail servers and over-flow inboxes.

- Emails that warn of a new virus that causes irreversible, improbable damage are usually hoaxes.

- Some hoaxes advise the removal of specific programs—programs that are not viruses but are vital for the operation of your computer.

- Don't forward email warnings without confirming the existence of the virus.

Section IV: Supporting Computer Networks

Troubleshooting networks

Once found only in large business environments, networks are now common in small businesses and even homes. Because of their complexity, networks are a source of problems. Installing a suitable network can avoid many service calls. With so many types of networking connections and devices available, network choices can be overwhelming. Helping the user install a secure, reliable network that meets current and future needs reduces service requests and maintenance calls.

A network is two or more computers connected to share resources. File sharing, print sharing, email, Internet access, schedule sharing, centralized security, and access to central data files are the main reasons to set up a network.

- Peer-to-peer networks assign equivalent responsibilities to each computer on the network. Each computer is considered a node on the network. Current Windows computers can be joined easily in peer-to-peer networks.

- Client-server networks dedicate one computer, usually a powerful one, to manage disk drives, printers, and communication traffic. Client computers, or workstations, rely on the server for access to files, devices, and resources.

- Local area networks (LAN) connect computers in a single building or small area.

- Metropolitan area networks (MAN) connect computers with high-speed connections in a town or city.

- Wide area networks (WAN) use long-range communication links to connect networks over long distances.

Choosing a network topology

A physical network topology describes the shape of a network and how the computers are connected together.

- Star topology connects all devices to a central hub. All nodes communicate with each other and to other networks by passing data through the hub.

- Bus topology connects all devices on the network to a central cable or bus.

- Ring topology connects each computer to two other computers until all the computers are joined in a ring or continuous loop.

- Mesh topology connects every computer or node in the network to every other node.

- Hybrid topology combines two or more of the other basic physical topologies into one network.

Identifying network protocols

Computers require a standard method of communicating or protocol so they can understand each other. Many protocols exist, but only a few are currently in use.

- Transmission Control Protocol/Internet Protocol (TCP/IP) is a suite or collection of protocols used by the Internet and other network systems.

- NetBIOS Enhanced User Interface (NetBEUI) was popular with older Windows systems and lacked the flexibility of TCP/IP.

- Internetwork Packet Exchange/Sequenced Packet Exchange (IPX/SPX) is a networking protocol used by Novell Netware operating systems.

Installing a Network Interface Card (NIC)

Computers require hardware to communicate with each other over a network. Each network card has a permanent, unique MAC address burned into the hardware to distinguish the card from every other card on the network.

- Internal NIC adapters are inserted into one of the peripheral slots in the computer. Many computer system boards have built-in Ethernet connections so no additional hardware is required.

- PCMCIA cards can connect portable computers to the network. Portables may come with built-in network connections.

- Parallel port adapters require special software and are not standard network devices.

Table 4.1: Home office options

Characteristic	Phone lines	Power lines	Ethernet
Medium	Installed phone lines	Installed power lines	New twisted pair or fiber optic cables
Connection	PCI card or USB adapter to phone socket	Parallel, USB, or Ethernet connection to wall outlet adapter	Often PCI card to hub or router
Cost	About $60 per device	About $40 per device	About $30 plus cables
Speed	10 Mbps	14 Mbps	100 Mbps to 1,000 Mbps

Connecting the computers to the network

The four popular options for creating a home or small office network transmit data through phone lines, power lines, Ethernet cables, or via radio waves. **Table 4.1** on the previous page compares the first three options, while a variety of wireless options are compared in **Table 4.2**. Prices and speed are typical, but a wide variety of options are available.

All networks allow the user to share a printer between computers, share a single Internet connection, exchange files, play multi-player games, and stream data to other computers. Each type of network has specific advantages and disadvantages that you must consider. Different manufacturers improve certain features.

Table 4.2: *WLAN and WPAN characteristics*

Characteristic	Bluetooth	
Transmission medium	Radio frequency (RF)	
Range	10 cm to 100 m	
Speed	To 1 Mbps	
Applications	Notebooks, desktops, and handheld computers; phones and pagers, modems, LAN access devices, and headsets	
Security	Provides authentication and encryption	
Advantage	Can transmit through solid, non-metal objects	

- Phone line networks are inexpensive, easy to install, stan-
dardized, compatible and reliable, require a phone connection for each device, fast, work with Macs and older
Windows machines, and don't require hubs or routers.

- Power line networks are inexpensive, use existing wiring usually found in every room, are very fast, and are
easy to install.

- Ethernet is a universally accepted business standard
that uses readily available components with proven
reliability.

Working with wireless networks

The four types of wireless local area networks (WLANs)
and wireless personal area networks (WPANs) used are

IrDA	HomeRF	Wi-Fi (WECA, 802.11)
Infra-red light	RF	RF
Short range 0–1 meter	23 to 38m	To 305m
9600 bps to 16 Mbps	1 Mbps to 2 Mbps	Up to 11 Mbps
Notebooks, desktops, and handheld comput-ers; printers, phones, pagers, modems, cameras, LAN access devices, and industrial equipment	Home networks	Business networks
Short-range and narrow angle of IrDA provides a simple form of security	Provides data encryption	Provides authentica-tion and encryption
World-wide acceptance	Allows up to 120 devices	Fast, reliable, long range, and supports wireless standards

Bluetooth, IrDA, HomeRF, and Wi-Fi (WECA or 802.11), as shown in **Table 4.2**. When installing a new network, it is often cost-effective to install a wireless network instead of a hard-wired cable network because wireless networks require no cables.

Wi-Fi is now a common option on laptops. Internet cafes, airline waiting rooms, and public places are installing base stations or access points to attract visitors. Wi-Fi is available in several formats, as shown in **Table 4.3**, and not all formats are compatible.

The faster and more secure the network, the more it will cost. Choose a network that is compatible with current equipment and work practices. The items below will help you discuss wireless networks with your customers:

- In ad-hoc mode, each client communicates directly with other clients on the network.

- In infrastructure mode, each client sends its communications to a central station Access Point (AP) which acts as an Ethernet bridge and forwards the communications onto the network.

- A client can exchange data over the network only after it moves through three steps to set up a relationship

Table 4.3: *Popular Wi-Fi options*

	802.11b	802.11g	WiMax
Maximum speed	11 MBps	54 MBps	70 MBps
Typical maximum range	150 feet	150 feet	30 miles
Users per antenna	32	64	Thousands
Base station cost	$60–$100	$100–$150	Not yet available

or Association: unauthenticated and unassociated to authenticated and unassociated to authenticated and associated.

Working with Ethernet networks

Ethernet networks are still the most common networks you will have to support. Other networks are rapidly evolving and often use proprietary hardware and software. Ethernets are standard and easily combine hardware from many manufacturers. An Ethernet network requires a card or connection in each computer, and cables or some other way of transmitting data from the computer to the rest of the network. **Table 4.4** lists the characteristics of commonly used cables.

Unshielded Twisted Pair (UTP) cables are sets of twisted pairs of 22 or 24 AWG solid wires in an insulated jacket.

Table 4.4: *Characteristics of cables*

Cable	Characteristics
Coaxial cable	Medium capacity. Ethernet systems (10 MBps) and Arcnet. More costly than UTP. More difficult to terminate. More resistant to interference than UTP. Bending can cause problems.
Twisted pair (STP and UTP)	Inexpensive. Easy to terminate. Susceptible to interference. Capacity is low to medium. Medium to high signal loss.
Fiber optic	Comparatively expensive. High capacity. Immune to electro magnetic interference. Low loss. Connectors are expensive and more difficult to install. Long distance with low loss.

Some locations may require Shielded Twisted Pair (STP), characterized by a braided wire around all the other wires to reduce unwanted interference. UTP and STP cables use RJ-45 connectors and, as shown in **Table 4.5**, are available in several categories.

When looking down with the cable extending away from you and the pins pointing down, pin one is to the extreme left of the RJ-45 connector. Following standard

Table 4.5: *Categories of twisted pair cables*

Category	Typical usage	Speed	Description
1	Voice only	Not applicable	Traditional telephone cable
2	Voice and data	Up to 4 Mbps	Usually includes four twisted pair wires
3	Voice and data	Up to 10 Mbps	Usually includes four twisted pair wires, at three twists per foot
4	Voice and data	Up to 20 Mbps	Usually includes four twisted pair wires
5	Voice and data	Up to 100 Mbps	Usually includes four twisted pair copper wires
5e	Voice and data	Up to 1 Gbps	Usually includes four twisted pair copper wires
6	Voice and data	Up to 1.2 Gbps (possible theoretical speeds of up to 2.5 Gbps)	Usually includes four twisted pair copper wires
7	Voice and data	Projected up to 4 to 10 Gbps	Under development, but expected to include four shielded twisted pair copper wires

wiring procedures in **Table 4.6** makes maintenance and replacement easier.

Coaxial cable is a single-conductor, copper-core cable, surrounded by insulation, a layer of metallic foil, and then the outer plastic jacket. Coaxial cables use BNC connectors and are available in several grades, known as Radio Grade (RG), as listed in **Table 4.7**.

You can use the information in **Table 4.8** and **Table 4.9**, both on the next page, to help you make the correct

Table 4.6: *Categories of twisted-pair cables*

Pin	Wire color combination EIA/TIA-568A	Wire color combination EIA/TIA-568B
1	White/Green	White/Orange
2	Green/White	Orange/White
3	White/Orange	White/Green
4	Blue/White	Blue/White
5	White/Blue	White/Blue
6	Orange/White	Green/White
7	White/Brown	White/Brown
8	Brown/White	Brown/White

Table 4.7: *Grades of coaxial cables*

Radio grade	Description
RG6	Used for surveillance cameras and other video devices.
RG8	52-ohm cable used for thicknet Ethernet networks.
RG58	50-ohm cable used for thinnet Ethernet networks. RG58/U uses a stranded copper wire core. RG58A/U uses a solid copper core wire.
RG59	75-ohm cable used for cable television (CATV).
RG62	93-ohm cable used for ARCNET networks.

physical connections on your network. As you can see, each type of cable puts specific limits on the maximum network segment.

Cable installation is an expensive and time-consuming activity, so it should be done correctly the first time.

- Leave slack when installing cable so you can make changes later.

- Test your installation at each step so it's always working.

- Avoid running cables near fluorescent lights and sources of electrical interference.

- Protect the cable from physical damage.

- Label both ends of each cable.

Table 4.8: *Comparison of network cables and topologies*

Common name	Description	Type	Topology	
10BaseT	Common	Twisted pair	Star	
10Base2	ThinNet	Coaxial	Bus	
10Base5	ThickNet	Coaxial	Bus	
100BaseT	Common	Twisted pair	Star	

Table 4.9: *High-speed Ethernet connections*

Bus	Data rate	Type	
10BaseF	10 Mbps	Fiber	
100BaseT	100 Mbps	Balanced	
100BaseF	100 Mbps	Fiber	
Gigabit Ethernet	1000 Mbps	Fiber or 1000BaseT	

- Use cable ties (not tape) to keep cables in the same location together.

The cable from the computer usually leads to another device, rather than to another computer. The network devices vary in sophistication and function.

- Hubs distribute network information through connectors to all attached computers.

- Switchboxes manage the flow of information and work more effectively than a hub.

- Bridges allow different types of networks to communicate. Bridges can boost the signal so computers can communicate over longer distances.

- Gateways connect a smaller network to a larger one. Often, that large network is the Internet.

Connector	Segment	Speed
RJ-45	0.5 to 100 meters	10 Mbps
BNC	185 meters	10 Mbps
BNC	500 meters	10 Mbps
RJ-45	5 to 100 meters	100 Mbps

Description	Topology
2000 meters	Point-to-Point
100 meters, category 5 cable	Multi-Point
2000 meters	Point-to-Point
Uses Fiber Channel or EIA568 CAT5	Point-to-Point

- Routers examine each piece of incoming data and pass it on to the computer that requested it. A wireless access point acts like a router to wireless computers.

Inside TCP/IP

While there are many network protocols in use today, TCP/IP has emerged as the *de facto* standard. When you set up a computer to support TCP/IP, you need to configure the addresses described below:

- IP address is a unique 32-bit number that identifies a specific sender or receiver of information on the Internet. Part of the IP (Internet Protocol), the number identifies both the network and the particular device on that network that is sending or receiving information.

- Subnet mask is a binary number that is combined with the IP address using a bitwise AND operation so the administrator can isolate the subnet portion of the address from the full IP address. The mask is a binary number the same length as the IP address, but the mask contains 1s in the binary locations of the data that must be isolated from the IP address, and 0s in the locations where the data may be ignored.

Table 4.10: *IP address classes, where x represents a network value and y represents a host value*

	IP address in binary format			
Class A	0xxxxxxx	yyyyyyyy	yyyyyyyy	yyyyyyyy
Class B	10xxxxxx	xxxxxxxx	yyyyyyyy	yyyyyyyy
Class C	110xxxxx	xxxxxxxx	xxxxxxxx	yyyyyyyy
Class D	1110xxxx	reserved	reserved	reserved
Class E	1111xxxx	reserved	reserved	reserved

- Default gateway is used if no specific gateway is specified. A gateway translates between different protocols so computers on a variety of connected networks can exchange data.

- DNS server addresses are the IP addresses of computer servers that translate domain names from the .com format to the binary IP address required by devices on the Internet. The Domain Name System (DNS) is a huge, distributed, database spread across many computers that work together to find the IP address for any domain name used on the Internet.

As shown in **Table 4.10**, Class A, Class B, and Class C public IP addresses can be assigned to individuals and organizations; Class D and Class E IP addresses are reserved and aren't used on the public Internet.

If you want to create an intranet or private IP network, you must use address ranges listed in **Table 4.11**. These non-routable addresses won't conflict with IP addresses on the public Internet.

Table 4.11: *IP address blocks for private networks*

	Start address	End address
Class A	10.0.0.0	10.255.255.255
Class B	172.16.0.0	172.31.255.255
Class C	192.168.0.0	192.168.255.255

Number of networks	Number of hosts
2^7 or 128	2^{24} or 16,777,216
2^{14} or 16,384	2^{16} or 65,536
2^{21} or 2,097,152	2^8 or 256
N/A	N/A
N/A	N/A

There are several IP addresses that you should never assign to a host on an IP network. As described below, these include the default route address, the loopback address, the network address, and the broadcast address:

- **0.0.0.0.** This address is known as the default route address. By definition, it refers to the Internet as a single entity.

- **127.0.0.1.** This address is known as the loopback address and refers to the local host. Packets sent to this address never go out on the network; instead, they're "looped back" to the local machine.

- **w.x.y.0.** This address is known as the network address. It ends in all binary zeros and is used to refer to the network as a whole. For example, instead of writing a range of IP addresses as 192.168.1.0–192.168.1.255, you can refer to the entire network as 192.168.1.0.

- **w.x.y.255.** This address is known as the broadcast address. It ends in all binary ones, which is the same as decimal 255. For example, 192.168.1.255 represents the broadcast address for the 192.168.1.0 network.

Microsoft Windows operating systems offer several tools for troubleshooting connectivity on TCP/IP networks. The tools you'll use most often include:

- ipconfig shows the network settings for the computer.

- ping shows whether the computer can reach a given IP address.

- winipcfg shows your current TCP/IP network protocol settings.

- tracert shows a network packet being sent and received and the amount of hops required for that packet to get to its destination.

- nslookup shows the IP address or hostname of a machine.

Networks are prone to multiple problems because of the amount of hardware and software that must be functioning correctly.

- Check the network settings, the TCP/IP settings, and the user settings if a user cannot connect to the network.

- Secure any loose cables connections, reseat loose adapter cards, and replace any defective cables if users occasionally lose their network connections.

- Authorize the user to have access to resources, and make sure the resources are functional, if a user has a problem accessing resources over the network.

Setting up a Windows XP network

To install a network, you must choose the best technology for the situation, plan the layout and connections, buy and install the hardware, and then configure the software so all the components exchange data reliably. Software setup using the Windows XP Network Setup Wizard follows the procedures summarized in **Table 4.12** on the next page.

User accounts identify who is permitted to use the network and what options are available to them. To create a new user account, the network administrator performs the steps in **Table 4.13**, also on the next page.

Windows XP has a system of folders that make file sharing and protection easy to accomplish. The following instructions are specific to Windows XP, but other operating systems have similar capabilities.

• Guarantee a file is always available to all users of that machine by placing it in the Windows XP Shared Directory.

Table 4.12: *Steps for configuring a network*

Step	Procedure
Start the Wizard	Launch the Network Setup Wizard from My Network Places or Network Connections.
Select a connection method	Indicate if the computer connects directly to the Internet or connects through another computer or gateway.
Select the Internet connection	Choose or let the Wizard select your Internet connection. Connection options may include a dial-up connection or an Ethernet connection.
Give the computer a name and description	Choose a unique computer name. Some Internet connections require a specific name.
Name the network	Enter a network name that matches the network name for other computers on the same network.
Create setup disk	Create a disk that can establish compatible network settings on all other computers on the network.
Share files	Select the folder containing the file and choose File | Sharing and Security to set the sharing needed for the file. File and Print Sharing capability is the default in Windows XP.
Share printers	Select the printer from Start | Settings | Printers and Faxes and choose File | Sharing to set the desired sharing characteristics.

- Share entire drives and individual folders over a network by right-clicking on the chosen item, selecting Sharing and Security, and choosing the settings for the desired amount of sharing.

- Protect a file from other users by placing it in your user profile folder in the Documents and Settings directory, and by making that directory or subdirectory private in the Sharing and Security options.

Troubleshooting Internet connectivity

An Internet connection is now standard for most home and office networks. Availability and cost often determine the type of connection used.

Choosing an Internet connection

There are several ways you can connect a single computer or a private network to the public Internet. The list below and on the next page describes the most common methods.

- Local area networks connect computers that are physically close to each other. If the LAN has a connection to

Table 4.13: Steps for creating a new user

Step	Procedure
Start the User Accounts Control Panel	Select Start	Settings	Control Panel	User Accounts.
Enter a new account	Select Create a New Account, rather than edit an account or change logon procedures.
Name the account	Choose a recognizable name suitable for welcome screens and the Start menu.
Select the account type	Choose an administrator account to give the user total control over the machine, or select Limited so the user can access only his own files or files in the Shared Directory.

the Internet, then computers on the LAN will be able to access the Internet.

- Digital Subscriber Line (DSL) allows high-speed transmission (typical speed is 1.5 Mbps) of digital data over regular copper telephone lines. Users must be close to a telephone-central office to reach the Internet with DSL.

- Digital Satellite System (DSS) connects at 400 Kbps. Some satellite systems are download only, and require a dial-up connection for uploading.

- Cable requires a cable digital modem connected to a TV coaxial cable to provide access to the Internet with a typical speed of 1.5 Mbps.

- Integrated Services Digital Network (ISDN) transmits data at a rate up to 128 Kbps over ordinary telephone copper wire.

- Dial-up connections use analog modems and Plain Old Telephone Service (POTS) to reach the Internet at speeds up to 56 Kbps.

- Satellite requires a dish antenna aimed at a specific geo-stationary satellite so it can send and often receive data from the Internet.

- Wireless uses radio waves to carry data (without wires) over some part of a wireless Internet connection.

Sharing an Internet connection
Once an Internet connection is brought into a location, more than one computer can use that single connection. A single computer can be used as an Internet server, or additional hardware can direct Internet traffic.

- A router forwards packets of data along networks. Several computers might connect to a router using Ethernet connections, forming a local area network. The router (sometimes called a gateway) might connect to the cable modem or other Internet connection and let all the connected computers access the Internet through that one connection.

- Microsoft ICS is an Internet Connection Sharing capability that is built into Windows software. ICS allows other users on a network to connect to the Internet through a single computer. The network administrator can set up ICS using the Network Wizard or Network Connections options.

Securing network communications

Insecure Internet connections allow intruders to steal data from computers on the network. Security devices must be installed to protect the network from hackers.

- Firewalls are software or hardware systems that prevent unauthorized access to or from a private network. A firewall can inspect all messages entering or leaving the Internet from the network, and block all messages that do not meet previously established criteria. Routers have built-in hardware firewalls that can, if selected, protect users on the network. Windows XP has built-in firewall capabilities.

- VPNs, or Virtual Private Networks, use encryption and other security features so only authorized users can exchange information over the network. The actual data may be transmitted over the public Internet, but only members of VPN can send and receive data on the VPN.

Data encryption is the process of putting your data into a secret code that only you or those you designate can understand. To read encrypted or ciphered text, you need a key or password to decrypt or decode it. The encrypted data is only as secure as the secrecy of the key.

- Different software packages encrypt data using different techniques. Some programs encrypt individual files, and some encrypt entire folders. Some programs never store unencrypted data on the disk, but only in RAM.

- Wireless technology broadcasts radio signals that hackers can pick up. All communications using wireless technology should be encrypted.

- Verify you have a secure Internet connection before transmitting any personal or financial information over the Internet.

Password hackers, or crackers, have sophisticated programs to help them discover your secret passwords. Although most passwords can be found eventually, the more difficult it is to figure out your password, the more likely the crackers will move on to easier targets. Windows XP users should change their passwords at regular intervals in the User Accounts Control Panel.

- Use the maximum number of characters allowed in your password.

- Mix upper- and lowercases at random in your password.

- Mix digits and punctuation if they are permitted.

- Never use a word or name that appears in a book or dictionary.

- Easy to remember passwords are still possible, such as 8Spud4Din, 2Gud2B4goT, and other "vanity plate" creations.

Section V: Customer Care

As a computer service professional, it's important for you to achieve and maintain customer satisfaction by providing good service at a reasonable cost and in a timely fashion. Let's take a look at some fundamental customer service concepts to help you measure your effectiveness. We'll examine some guidelines for demonstrating professional conduct and we'll discuss some of the expectations your customers have, as well. Lastly, we'll describe some techniques for improving your communication skills.

Professional conduct

You're a representative of your profession, as well as your company. The way you conduct yourself professionally directly influences the satisfaction of your customer. Think about the kind of professional you want to be. What do you expect of yourself? What traits do you expect of a service provider?

Professional traits

A good rule to follow is to treat your customer the way you'd want to be treated under similar circumstances. When gauging your own professional conduct, you may want to consider the following traits and their respective examples:

- **Acceptance.** Be non-judgmental about your customer's level of computer competence, choice of hardware, personal traits, and environmental conditions.

- **Competence.** Instill confidence and credibility in your customers by demonstrating your skills and, when necessary, stating the limits of your knowledge.

- **Courtesy.** Be polite and friendly on the phone and in person; address your customer as sir or ma'am; use titles, such as Dr., Mr., or Ms., with last names; and ask permission before entering your customer's personal space.

- **Dependability.** Be there when you say you will, keep your promises or let the customer know of any changes, work efficiently and accurately, be prepared with the right equipment, and don't make promises you can't keep.

- **Flexibility.** Work around the customer's time and space demands, think on your feet, apply what you've previously learned, try alternate solutions, and ask for help when you need it.

- **Honesty.** Tell the truth about needed repairs, costs, and time estimates; be honest about your level of expertise and make professional referrals when appropriate; and promptly admit your errors.

- **Patience.** Be patient with angry customers, computer-illiterate customers, baffling equipment, unavoidable delays, and frustrating policies and procedures.

- **Punctuality.** Be on time, call if you'll be detained, and make follow-up calls as promised.

Professional behavior

Your work environment may be in a repair shop, at a help desk, or onsite. Whatever the situation, you'll want to present a neat, clean, business-like appearance. Onsite work may take you into many settings, from muffler repair shops to executive offices. You may be asked to remove your shoes or put on a hard hat. Be aware of the corporate culture, and respond accordingly. Be sure to keep your work area neat. Don't pile materials on your coworker's books and files. Clean up after yourself; a customer may chase after you with the anti-static bag you left behind. When onsite, ask where to dispose of materials; find out where the recycling bin is for printer test run paper. The following are some key facets of professional behavior you'll want to demonstrate:

- **Accountability.** Don't misrepresent your credentials, competence, or training. Take responsibility for your actions and admit your mistakes. In questions of a conflict of interest between your company and the customer, refer to your supervisor or follow your company's procedures. Be aware of your company's policy on accepting gifts or samples, and on socializing with customers.

- **Confidentiality.** Many fields, including medicine, social work, and special education, are regulated by state laws concerning the confidentiality of their clients. All companies have personal information about their employees. Many corporations have sensitive information about the development of their products or services. Treat any information you learn about your customer's business as confidential. Know your company's policies concerning confidential information and follow them.

- **Ethics.** You have an obligation to take responsibility for the ethical conduct in your delivery of service. The issues involved are complex and ever-changing in the relatively young computer industry. An unethical practice may become so routine that it's falsely assumed to be acceptable behavior. Learn your company's policies and adhere to them.

- **Legal compliance.** Software copyright infringement, or pirating, concerns the legal issues surrounding the distribution and use of software. The Federal Copyright Act of 1976 protects the rights of the holder of the copyright. Usually a backup copy of software is allowed; a site license allows for multiple users at one facility. You're responsible for upholding the law by complying with the license agreement. Learn your company's policies and adhere to them.

- **Prioritization.** You'll often need to set priorities and make judgment calls. You'll recommend whether your customer should repair or replace equipment. You'll rank the urgency of your customers' needs. Base your decisions on common courtesy, fundamental fairness, and keeping promises.

Customer Expectations

Is the customer always right? No, the customer may be flat-out wrong at times. However, the customer is the bread and butter of your business. Rudeness is never an option. Challenge yourself to find the positive in every situation. Ask yourself: What is my job here? What are my obligations to the customer? What are my obligations to my employer?

Treat customers as you'd like to be treated

Since the customer is your reason for being a service technician, the customer deserves your acceptance and respect. The customer will have varying levels of computer experience, from novice to expert. He may be emotionally charged by the equipment problem, and you may become the target of anger or frustration.

You and the customer bring your own individual differences in values, beliefs, age, gender, personality, and communication styles. Whatever the circumstances, be sure to look beyond the immediate differences. Keep your focus on the person who needs your help. How can you provide it? Treat all of your customers as you'd like to be treated.

Your customers call because they need help, and they usually need it yesterday. Their sense of urgency is about deadlines and production; they may display frustration and anger. Remember, it's not about you; it's about their need to get back online as quickly as possible. Your best response is to be supportive, using the communication and problem-solving techniques listed in the following section. Be patient and honest; let the customer know that you're working toward a timely solution to the problem.

Communication skills

Next, let's take a look at some of the more important communication skills you'll need to develop as you provide service to your customers. Effective communication is undoubtedly the most important vehicle for establishing and maintaining good customer relations. As you read the following modes of communication, take some time to think about how you interact with your customers:

- **Active listening.** When your customer is describing the problem, listen actively to elicit as much information as you can. This technique may feel awkward at first, so try it out in a situation outside of your job. With practice, you'll use active listening skills more easily and creatively.

- **Agreeing with perception.** You can agree with the customer's perception of a situation without necessarily agreeing with what's said. As the customer realizes that you're not going to argue, he may see a safe place to begin solving the problem.

- **Conflict resolution.** You aim for customer satisfaction, and many times your interactions go smoothly. You may be greeted with: "Are we glad to see you!" When a customer specifically requests you, then you know you're doing something, or many things, right. Unfortunately, not all your interactions will be ideal. Your customer may be under stress for a number of reasons. Your customer may direct anger and frustration toward you. Remember, don't take the attack personally, and don't counter-attack. As a service provider, your job is to relieve some of the stress. Conflict resolution techniques can help you make a difference in customer satisfaction.

- **Empathy.** Let your customer know that you perceive and support what he is feeling. Try to be specific in naming the emotion and link it to the customer, using "you" not "I."

- **Eye contact.** You and your customer will make, maintain, and break eye contact as you talk with each other. When attention is directed to the problem at hand, eye contact may be minimal. You'll want to avoid staring directly at your customer—a form of invading personal space—or letting your gaze wander, indicating disinterest.

- **Finding a solution.** Together you and your customer can work out a specific plan for working through the problem. Brainstorm some ideas. Be careful about giving advice or solutions too early or too often in the process. Your job is to facilitate the decision-making process, which ultimately rests with the customer. Be sure to follow through with any commitments you make.

- **Forming an alliance.** Your customer needs to know that you're an ally, not an enemy. When the customer knows that you share his concerns, the problem-solving process can move forward. Give a sense of unity by using "we" instead of "you" or "I."

- **Gestures and facial expressions.** Gestures such as nodding, pointing, or measuring the air help expand the spoken message. Broad, friendly gestures indicate being open to the conversation, while sharp or jabbing gestures usually mean anger. The variety, intensity, and meaning of facial expressions are almost endless. You and your customer read each other's faces to gain insight into the spoken words. Your expression must match the content of your words; if they are mismatched, your customer will believe the message in your face rather than what you say.

- **Non-verbal clues.** Body language communicates more than actual words. Studies show that up to 70 percent of a message is conveyed through actions. Even when you're talking on the phone, non-verbal characteristics, such as tone of voice, add meaning to your message and help you interpret your customer's concerns.

- **Paraphrasing.** Restate what the customer says in your own words to make sure that you interpreted it correctly, to bring order to the customer's thoughts, and to relay that the message is important. Use statements, not questions, and don't add or change anything.

- **Passive listening**. Your message is: "I'm listening. Tell me more." You're alert, attentive, and accepting, but you don't participate actively in the conversation. Your silence may help your customer collect his thoughts, especially if he's upset or angry. Listen for factual data and be alert for feelings and attitudes, which are conveyed non-verbally. It may be difficult to keep from jumping in with a question or a "Yes, but…"; resist the temptation by writing down your thoughts to refer to later.

- **Positioning and posture.** Respect your customer's personal space. Depending on the circumstances, you may be from one and one-half to four feet away from your customer. If the customer backs up, you're too close. You may be working in close quarters; ask permission before you move into your customer's personal space. Messages are conveyed by body position. Slouching indicates, "I'm bored with this conversation." Holding your arms across the chest says, "I'm closed to what you're saying." Watch your body's signals, as well as those of your customer.

- **Questioning skills.** Ask questions to gain information, clarify what you have heard, and direct the conversation. Open-ended questions can elicit a lot of information. An example of an open-ended question is: "What happened after you pressed [Ctrl][Alt][Delete]?" Close-ended questions limit the amount of information by giving a choice of answers. An example of a close-ended question is: "What kind of printer do you have—laser or inkjet?" Yes/No questions further limit information exchange and can be used when you need to cut to the chase. An example of a yes/no question is: "Are you on a network?"

- **Reflecting feelings.** You can acknowledge what the customer is feeling without necessarily accepting the display of emotion. Check the customer's non-verbal messages, including tone of voice and facial expression. Be accurate and specific in naming the feeling. The feeling belongs to the customer, not you, so don't apologize for it.

- **Summarization.** Outline the main points of your conversation to summarize what has been said. You can begin the conversation by summarizing your understanding of the problem and then checking for clarification. During the conversation, you can re-establish the focus by listing the important facts. Bring closure by summing up the work performed. If a follow-up plan is needed, restate the responsibilities and timeline.

- **Timing.** You can set the pace of a conversation. A pause may be more valuable than an immediate answer, as it allows you time to formulate your response. If a situation escalates and your customer becomes agitated, you may ask him to slow down so that you can get all the information. When a customer is having difficulty ending a call to the help desk, you may gently step up the pace to indicate your need to move on.

- **Tone of voice.** The tone of voice indicates many internal moods: excitement, boredom, sarcasm, fear, or uncertainty. A rise in your voice at the end of a sentence makes it sound like a question, implying lack of assurance instead of competence. Listen to your customer's tone. Volume—loudness or softness—colors the spoken message. If your customer's agitation escalates, try lowering your volume to re-establish a sense of calm.

In the increasingly competitive world of business, it's more important than ever to provide superb customer service whenever possible. Regardless of whether you're supporting external or internal customers, customer satisfaction is the single-most important goal you should set for yourself.

Appendix

Working with number systems

Supporting computer systems often requires you to work with different number systems. The most common number systems are defined below and compared in **Table A.1**:

- **Binary.** Uses the digits 0 and 1 to represent the values 0 and 1, respectively.

- **Decimal.** Uses the digits 0–9 to represent the values 0–9, respectively.

- **Hexadecimal.** Uses the digits 0–9 to represent the values 0–9, and the letters A–F to represent the values 10–15, respectively.

Accessibility options

The Americans with Disabilities Act (ADA) has made computer accessibility for users with special needs a requirement. However, accessibility settings in Windows XP can also create problems for typical users because the function of common input devices and the screen display can be changed radically.

- Accessibility programs in the Accessories program group include Accessibility Wizard, Magnifier, Narrator, On-Screen Keyboard, and Utility Manager.

- Use the Accessibility Wizard to set the default text size, the scroll bar size, the icon size, the color scheme, cursor size and color, and the text insertion point blinking rate and width. The wizard also sets visual warnings in addition to sounds, sets captions, sets sticky keys for [Ctrl], [Alt], and [Shift], ignores repeated key strokes, plays sounds when [Caps Lock] key is pressed, displays extra keyboard help, duplicates mouse actions with the numeric key pad, changes the "handed-ness" of the mouse, sets the mouse speed, and determines who sees the accessibility options.

- Use the Magnifier option to magnify parts of the screen, Narrator to verbalize screen text and key presses, On-Screen Keyboard to enter letters using a mouse, and Utility Manager to control these programs.

Table A.1: *Common binary, decimal, and hexadecimal equivalents*

Decimal	Binary	Hexadecimal
0	0000 0000	00
1 or 2^0	0000 0001	01
2 or 2^1	0000 0010	02
3	0000 0011	03
4 or 2^2	0000 0100	04
5	0000 0101	05
6	0000 0110	06
7	0000 0111	07
8 or 2^3	0000 1000	08
9	0000 1001	09
10	0000 1010	0A
11	0000 1011	0B
12	0000 1100	0C
13	0000 1101	0D
14	0000 1110	0E
15	0000 1111	0F
16 or 2^4	0001 0000	10
32 or 2^5	0010 0000	20
64 or 2^6	0100 0000	40
128 or 2^7	1000 0000	80
256 or 2^8	1 0000 0000	01 00
512 or 2^9	10 0000 0000	02 00
1,024 or 2^{10}	100 0000 0000	04 00

About the Author

Joe Froehlich has contributed several articles to Element K Journals' IT Professional series. He's currently the editor of *Computer Support Professional* and *Mac Administration*, and he formerly managed the development of Element K's Solaris and Linux Professional courseware. You can contact Joe by sending an email to **apj@elementkjournals.com**.

Index

Numbers

A

B

C

H

I

M

Q

R

W

HELP US IMPROVE OUR COURSEWARE

Your comments are important to us. Please contact us at Element K Press LLC, 1-800-478-7788, 500 Canal View Boulevard, Rochester, NY 14623, Attention: Product Planning, or through our Web site at **http://support.elementkcourseware.com**

Web sites of interest

_____

_____

_____

_____

_____

_____

_____

_____

_____

_____

_____

_____

_____

_____

_____

_____

_____

_____

_____

_____

_____

_____

_____

Web sites of interest

_____

_____

_____

_____

_____

_____

_____

_____

_____

_____

_____

_____

_____

_____

_____

_____

_____

_____

_____

_____

_____

_____

Web sites of interest

_____

_____

_____

_____

_____

_____

_____

_____

_____

_____

_____

_____

_____

_____

_____

_____

_____

_____

_____

_____

_____

_____

_____

Web sites of interest

_____

_____

_____

_____

_____

_____

_____

_____

_____

_____

_____

_____

_____

_____

_____

_____

_____

_____

_____

_____

_____

_____

Notes

_____

_____

_____

_____

_____

_____

_____

_____

_____

_____

_____

_____

_____

_____

_____

_____

_____

_____

_____

_____

_____

_____

_____

Notes

_____

_____

_____

_____

_____

_____

_____

_____

_____

_____

_____

_____

_____

_____

_____

_____

_____

_____

_____

_____

_____

Notes

_____

_____

_____

_____

_____

_____

_____

_____

_____

_____

_____

_____

_____

_____

_____

_____

_____

_____

_____

_____

_____

_____

_____

Notes

Notes

_____

_____

_____

_____

_____

_____

_____

_____

_____

_____

_____

_____

_____

_____

_____

_____

_____

_____

_____

_____

_____

Notes

_____

_____

_____

_____

_____

_____

_____

_____

_____

_____

_____

_____

_____

_____

_____

_____

_____

_____

_____

_____

_____

_____

Notes

_____

_____

_____

_____

_____

_____

_____

_____

_____

_____

_____

_____

_____

_____

_____

_____

_____

_____

_____

_____

_____

_____

Notes

_____

_____

_____

_____

_____

_____

_____

_____

_____

_____

_____

_____

_____

_____

_____

_____

_____

_____

_____

_____

_____

_____

_____

Notes

_____

_____

_____

_____

_____

_____

_____

_____

_____

_____

_____

_____

_____

_____

_____

_____

_____

ACS21145 PG

0 99751 06749 3